Great Jewish Women

Profiles of Courageous Women
from the Maccabean Period to the Present

By Greta Fink

Published by:
MENORAH PUBLISHING COMPANY, INC.
and
BLOCH PUBLISHING COMPANY, INC.
New York, N.Y.

To my children
Deborah, Naomi and Benjamin
This book is lovingly dedicated

TABLE OF CONTENTS

List of Illustrations

Preface

Little is known about the contributions made by Jewish women throughout the ages. Either the historians pass them over, or, if they are outstanding figures in world history, the fact that they were Jewish is left unmentioned. It is the primary purpose of this work to sketch briefly those women who contributed to history and deserve to be better known as historical figures and as Jews. Perhaps this book will, in some way, counteract the cavalier treatment which the new *Encyclopedia Judaica* gives many of these great women; they are accorded just a passing mention or, at most, a very small article.

There have always been great Jewish women— throughout the ages and before today's modern Women's Liberation movement: the head of a free Judean State, a Talmudic scholar mentioned in the Talmud itself, a Hassidic rebbe, the foreign secretary of a European country, a genius in business and founder of an important industry, a Nobel Prize Laureate. They are just a few of the women described in this book. A woman who had the spark of greatness, ability and determination has always been able to succeed. As these short profiles further indicate, great women can be religious, areligious, antireligious, apostate, single, happily married, with children, childless, rich, poor, middle class, etc. In short, greatness is a quality in itself and to achieve greatness one does not need to shed or acquire any of the above-mentioned attributes.

As with men, some of these women are praiseworthy, others less so; some are tragic figures, others heroic. They are neither better nor worse than their male counterparts. They are their equals.

Queen Alexandra

It may come as a surprise to some people to learn that the Jews had a woman head of state before the renowned Golda Meir. In fact, there have been two female rulers of a Jewish nation before our own Mrs. Meir. The first, during the First Commonwealth, was the infamous daughter of Jezebel, the usurper Athalia (II Kings 11). The second, during the Second Commonwealth, was Salome Alexandra, the subject of this study.

The ruling House of the Second Commonwealth, the Hasmoneans, was founded by Mattathias, the son of Johanan, the son of Simon Hasmonai, a member of the priestly clan and his five sons. The first leader of this family was Judah the Maccabee. He was followed by his brother, Jonathan who in turn was followed by a third brother, Simon. Simon achieved complete independence from any foreign power in the year 142 B.C.E. (Before the Common Era, equivalent to before Christ in the English calendar). Simon was succeeded as high priest and ruler of Israel by his son Johanan Hyrcanus who ruled from 135-104 B.C.E.

When Hyrcanus died, according to his will his wife was charged with responsibility for the government and his eldest son, Judah Aristobulus, with the high priesthood. However, Aristobulus seized the government (104 B.C.E.), imprisoned his mother, and left her to die of starvation. He also imprisoned his brothers with the exception of Antigonus, his comrade-in-arms, whom he loved.

Judah Aristobulus had married Shalom Zion, later known as Salome Alexandra, sister, as the Talmud relates of Rabbi Simon ben Shetah, head of the Pharisees. In spite of this, however, the Pharisees were not happy with Aristobulus, a Sadducee, as he was the first of the Hasmoneans to take the title of king, a title which the Pharisees felt belonged only to the scion of the House of David.

Who were the Pharisees and their opponents, the Sadducees and what was their philosophy? The Sadducees believed only in the Written Word and did not hold any traditions as obligatory. They did not believe in fate or Providence but rather that events and human affairs are in our own power. Furthermore, they did not accept the concept of Resurrection, but taught that the soul died with the body. Theirs was the philosophy and political party of the military, the rich, and the aristocracy. It was only they who could afford to believe in self-determination, that one determines his own destiny, and that there is no other world after death. The poor and common man was precluded from both party and philosophy.

For the Pharisees, the Written Law was supplemented by the Oral Law, the traditions of the fathers, the words of the Scribes, and the measures introduced throughout the ages by the Rabbinic teachers. This made it a living religion. They believed in the Resurrection of the body and of a soul after death, in the Providential ordering of the affairs of man but not in determinism. For the Pharisees there was freedom of will and thus human accountability. Although their lives were a mixture of good and evil, in the future all would be good. This Kingdom of God would be realized with the coming of the Messiah.

The Jew who believes in a soul after death, must, to become worthy of the heavenly kingdom, perform good deeds and follow the Law which pertains to both his fellow man and his God. The Pharisaic religion brought comfort to the lowly, and their teachers were beloved by the common people. In the meeting houses or synagogues, they taught and preached the Torah, considered how man should conduct himself toward God and his fellow man, and fired the imagination with descriptions of the blessedness of the world to come. In the synagogues, the service was of the heart, of prayer and benediction. The synagogues became schools of virtue and from Palestine they soon spread to all of the Diaspora.

Aristobulus was a very sick man, having what was to prove within a year to be a fatal illness. Probably fearing a fate similar to that of her mother-in-law if Antigonus, brother of Aristobulus, were to become king, Salome Alexandra conspired to have Antigonus killed. Josephus relates that jealous courtiers told the king that his brother Antigonus was contemplating his murder and the assumption of the throne. At first Aristobulus refused to believe these stories. Then, at the Festival of Tabernacles, Antigonus returned from one of his military campaigns to pray at the Temple for the recovery of his brother who lay ill. It was reported to the sick king that Antigonus was in the Temple, in full military dress, with a strong body of troops. Aristobulus was now in doubt about his brother.

To resolve his uncertainty, he summoned Antigonus to the palace unarmed and ordered his bodyguards to allow Antigonus in if he obeyed. If, however, he came armed, he was to be killed immediately. Queen Alexandra reversed the message to say that the king had heard of his brother's fine new suit of armor and desired that Antigonus come arrayed in that armor so that he, the king, might see how magnificent it was. Antigonus complied with the latter message and was killed by the guards. When Aristobulus heard of his brother's death, he was so overcome that he suffered a hemorrhage and died soon after.

His widow, Salome, immediately gave orders for the release from prison of the king's three brothers. She appointed one of them, Alexander Jannai, as king and in accordance with Biblical law Alexander performed a levirate marriage as Salome was the widow of a childless brother. She was 37 years old while he was only 22.

Alexandra thought that she would be able to influence Alexander Jannai to change the favor of the Hasmoneans away from the Sadducees and toward the Pharisees, the party which her own brother headed. However, Jannai was unstable and headstrong and thought of and cared for nothing except military campaigns. Queen Alexandra could do nothing.

For 27 years Alexander Jannai fought foreign and civil wars and was extremely cruel to the Pharisees. They revolted against him, precipitating a civil war in which 50,000 Judeans were killed. Victorious, Jannai celebrated his victory by crucifying 800 Pharisees. Immediately afterward he again turned to foreign wars. During the final three years of his life, Jannai was afflicted with a debilitating fever and died while besieging Ragaba across the Jordan. Before his death, he appointed his wife, Alexandra, as head of the government, advising her to align herself with the Pharisees who were the party of the people. He further counselled her to give his body to the Pharisees to do with as they pleased. The Talmud (Sota 22a) related that Jannai sought to allay the queen's anxiety about the party strife rampant in Jerusalem, advising her "Do not fear either the true Pharisees or their honest opponents, but be on guard against the dyed ones (hypocrites) of both sides who act like Zimri and demand the reward of Phineas" (Numbers 25, 6-14).

This last political act of the king was his wisest, for the queen fully justified the confidence he had placed in her.

She was 64 years old at the time of her accession. Having spent the greater part of her adult life in an era of constant wars and internal violence, she was determined to bring peace and prosperity to her people. In this she succeeded magnificently and without detriment to the political relations of the Jewish state with the outside world. Alexandra received the reins of government at the camp before Ragaba and concealed the king's death until the fortress had fallen, in order that the seige might be maintained. Her next act was to ally herself with the Pharisees, who, having received assurances as to the queen's future policy, gave Alexander an honored burial due a king. She thus avoided any public affront to a dead king which would have had a divisive effect on the populace, as well as being fraught with danger to the Hasmonean dynasty.

The queen's accession brought freedom to hundreds whom Alexander had imprisoned in dungeons, and liberty to return home to thousands whom he had driven into exile. The Pharisees, who had suffered untold misery under Alexander Jannai, now became not only a tolerated part of the community but actually the ruling class. Alexandra appointed her eldest son Hyrcanus II, a peaceful man wholly in sympathy with the Pharisees, as high priest. The Sanhedrin was reorganized in accordance with the Pharisees' wishes. Formerly this body was a sort of "House of Lords," the members of which belonged to the aristocracy and were subservient to the king. From Alexandra's time on, the Sanhedrin became a "supreme court" for the administration of justice and religious matters under the guidance of the Pharisees. Thus, the reign of Alexandra marks an important epoch in the history of Jewish internal government.

The Pharisees, who now assumed control of affairs of state, were determined to be avenged for the death of their 800 brethren. They therefore petitioned the queen to destroy all who had helped Jannai in this horrible massacre. As a result, Diogenes, leader of the Sadducees and prime mover in that barbarous act, was killed, inspiring fear among the rest of the Sadducees. A deputation led by Aristobulus II, Alexandra's other son, petitioned her for help. They asked to be allowed to live outside Jerusalem in various fortresses, implying that if she refused they would join hostile neighboring kings as mercenaries. In her desire to avoid all party conflict, Alexandra granted their requests. However, the most important fortresses of Hyrcania, Alexandrion, and Machaerus, she did not entrust to them.

Acting with prudence in foreign affairs, Alexandra increased the size of the army and carefully provisioned numerous fortified places. She avoided all military expeditions except one, led by her son Aristobulus II against Damascus, which was without result. When threatened by the King of Armenia, she kept him away from Judea by sending him gifts. She made no alliances and kept Judea completely independent.

Throughout this period, Judea enjoyed unparalleled prosperity. The Talmud relates that during Alexandra's rule, as a reward for her piety, rain fell only on Friday nights so that the working class lost no pay because of rain falling during their working time. The fertility of the soil was so great that grains of wheat grew as large as kidney beans, oats as large as olives, and lentils as large as gold denarii (Ta'anit 23a). Alexandra's nine year reign was considered a time of peace and prosperity. She died in her seventy-third year of life.

After her death, catastrophe struck. Although Alexandra had chosen John Hyrcanus II to succeed her as king, his brother Aristobulus declared war and defeated him in battle. A peace was arranged and an accomodation was effected whereby Aristobulus II, the younger, more ambitious and energetic man, became king while Hyrcanus, a peace-loving and private-minded individual, became high priest. However, the people and groups behind these two men were irreconcilable and a continuous battle raged, with the result that Judea lost her independence to Rome. The Hasmonean dynasty came to an end and an Idumean, Herod, a Roman lackey, ascended the throne. It was a disaster in every respect.

Alexandra has been severely censured by historians for her lack of statesmanship, for being interested in peace even at the cost of detriment to the state, for not uniting the Judean people but rather sowing the seeds of conflict, and for not seeking to settle the differences between the Sadducees and the Pharisees. She is further criticized for not deciding between her two sons. In dividing the power, giving one the high priesthood and the other the fortresses, she insured civil war and eventual loss of independence. In short, she is judged a temporary success but an everlasting failure. Is this assessment correct? What kind of person was she?

It is fairly obvious that Salome Alexandra must have been a very beautiful and charming woman. Although not of royal blood, she married the crown prince and eventual king. Her marriage probably took place at an early age and it must have been agony for her to be married at least 10 to 15 years without offspring. In the last year of her husband's life her instinct for self-preservation caused her to have her brother-in-law killed, and being childless she was compelled to appoint the best of a bad bunch as the future king and her husband-to-be. Again her position must have been quite insecure until the birth of her sons. At the age of 37, never having had children, her births must have been considered a minor miracle.

Although much older than her husband, King Jannai, she was nevertheless able to retain his respect and devotion, no mean accomplishment as he was an unstable and cruel man. She had to stand aside while Jannai persecuted the Pharisees, her brother's religious party and the one she herself favored, throughout the 27 years of his reign. Then after his death, she, a woman of 64, an advanced age in those days, had the leadership of the nation thrust upon her.

What was the condition of this nation? It had been racked by both foreign and civil wars for years. The people were sorely divided between parties which had both political and religious differences. The state of the economy was bad. Foreign dangers were ever present. How did she cope? In a word, brilliantly. There was unprecedented peace and prosperity: no wars, foreign or civil, no conflicts, no entangling alliances. No one contests this. What, then, about the charges against her?

Certainly she was for peace. After 27 years of constant bloodshed, who can blame her? But the charge "to the detriment of the state," is false. She had peace because she was strong. It was not a peace achieved at the price of subservience or weakness.

That she was interested in the present at the expense of the future, that she did not settle the discord between the Sadducees and Pharisees, that she did not choose between her sons, thus sowing the seeds of a future disastrous civil war—in truth, all that is correct. However, she did better than anyone else in quieting the dissension between the two parties. It is naive to think that in nine short years a conflict which had been simmering for decades could be settled. Had her reign lasted 25 years, there might have been a chance to resolve it. As for not choosing between her sons, she was unable to, because as a potential leader, each of them left much to be desired. This is obvious not only in light of later events, when both proved incredibly inept, but also by the fact that even the dying Jannai preferred his 64-year-old queen as ruler to either of his sons.

It is doubtful that picking one son over the other could have prevented Rome from conquering Judea with its subsequent loss of independence. Rome needed Judea to consolidate its Eastern empire. However, it is possible that even with Rome as the ruling power, the Hasmonean House might still have ruled Judea with better results for the people than Herod, his family, and outside procurators brought about. But this is conjecture. The odds are that the Roman procurators would have replaced the Hasmoneans even as they did the Herodeans and history would have taken its course.

A final judgment should determine that the reign of Salome Alexandra, with its unparalleled peace and prosperity, was equal, if not superior, to any during the Second Commonwealth.

Beruriah

The one discipline where it is rare and exceptional to find
women is Rabbinics. It is unusual to find a woman who can
understand Talmud, let alone become a recognized authority. Until recently, following the ruling of Maimonides,
as well as the renowned compilation of Jewish law, the
Shulhan Arukh, and other Rabbinc sources, Jewish girls were
not even permitted to study the subject. As a result, it is not
surprising that except for the daughter of Rashi and
perhaps one or two other women, there is no recorded instance in Jewish history since the early Middle Ages of
Jewish women ever having mastered the Talmudic text.
However, in Mishnaic times (c. 30 B.C.E.—220 C.E.) there
were women who were educated in this field. One of these
women was a recognized authority the equal of most of our
Tannaic scholars.

Beruriah was born in Israel in the first quarter of the
second century. The daughter of Rabbi Hananiah ben
Teradion, one of the "10 martyrs" about whom we read on
Yom Kippur, she was also the wife of Rabbi Meir, one of
the greatest Tannaim and one of the most outstanding Rabbinic scholars in our history.

This was an historic and tragic period in Jewish history.
In 117 C.E., Hadrian became the Roman emperor and
some time after, issued two laws which affected the Jews

sorely. He wanted Jerusalem converted into a heathen city. Furthermore, he forbade the mutilation of the body, thereby prohibiting circumcision. Although these decrees were not aimed at the Jews specifically, in effect they were an attack on the Jewish religion and were met with violent resistance. The spiritual leader of this third and final war against Rome was the saintly scholar, Rabbi Akiba. The military leader was Simon of Cozeba, more popularly known as Bar Kokheba (son of the star).

The insurrection broke out in 132 C.E., although preparations had been going on in secret for some time. It spread throughout Palestine and Jews from the entire diaspora came to fight on the side of their brethren. At first Bar Kokheba defeated every Roman general sent to oppose him, and for two years, 132-134 C.E., governed an independent kingdom which he commemorated by the minting of coins. Finally Hadrian was forced to dispatch his best general, Severus, from Britain where he was subduing another rebellion. By the brilliant strategy of attacking the Jews piecemeal and avoiding a pitched battle, Hadrian was able to exhaust and finally reduce the Jewish army. Severus's final victory came at Beth-Ther where Bar Kokheba was killed and all effective resistance ceased. The Jews lost over half a million men, while thousands of others were sold as slaves. The Romans also suffered severe losses so that Hadrian was forced to eliminate from his victory message to the Senate the usual statement, "I and the army are well."

Judea was not in ruins. Jerusalem was rebuilt by Hadrian as a pagan city where Jews were now prohibited entry. They were also forbidden not only circumcision but the observance of the Sabbath and all other religious practices. Most vicious and cruel, the teaching of the Torah and the ordination or the graduation of rabbis was proscribed. In a secret meeting, the surviving teachers of the Jewish Law ruled that as far as the general population was concerned, their primary concern was survival to await better days. Accordingly, to avoid death and torture, as the Romans had spies and informers everywhere, all laws except the most important, i.e., murder, adultery and idolatry, might be broken. For themselves, however, the rabbis adopted a stricter stance and were eventually martyred.

Beruriah was born in these traumatic times. She had a brother very close in age to herself and a younger sister. Both she and her brother were brilliant students and while quite young were considered authorities on difficult questions of Jewish Law. It is related in the Tosefta (Kelim B.K. 4:9) that on a particular point of law, Rabbi Halafta queried Simon ben Hananiah who in turn applied to the children of Rabbi Hananiah ben Teradion for the answer. Beruriah's brother answered one way, while his sister answered it differently. When Judah ben Baba, another Mishnaic scholar, heard of these differing opinions, he remarked, "Hananiah's daughter teaches better than his son."

Beruriah was a model to whom all students could aspire; she was the yardstick by which their abilities were measured. The Talmud (Pesahim 62b) relates that Rabbi Simlai asked Rabbi Johanan to teach him the particularly difficult Book of Genealogies. Rabbi Johanan refused at first, consenting at last only after repeated requests. "Teach it to me in three months," Rabbi Simlai urged, whereupon Rabbi Johanan became angry and said, "If Beruriah, who was able to learn 300 laws from 300 teachers in one day, nevertheless took three years to learn the Book of Genealogies, where did you get the absurd idea that you could do it in three months?"

Beruriah's brother, incidentally, later led a dissolute life and fell in with a band of robbers, a reaction perhaps due partly to the fact that he was outshone in his studies by his exceptional sister. One day he betrayed his fellow conspirators' secret to the authorities and in revenge, they killed him and filled his mouth with dust and pebbles. The people wanted to give him a proper funeral and pronounce a eulogy out of respect to his father, but the latter would not permit it. Rabbi Hananiah insisted that he himself would say what had to be said concerning his son, and he opened with the text, "Neither have I harkened to the voice of my teachers nor inclined mine ear to them that instructed me. I was well nigh in all evil in the midst of the congregation and assembly" (Prov. 5:13 f.). His mother spoke next and quoted the following passage: "A foolish son is vexation to his father and bitterness to her that bore him" (Prov. 17:25). Obviously his mother must have been quite learned herself. His sister Beruriah concluded with: "Bread of falsehood is sweet to a man, but afterwards his mouth shall be filled with gravel stone" (Prov. 20:17)

The Talmud relates that Beruriah was expert in all phases of learning, both in Halakhah (Jewish law) and in Biblical exegesis. In addition to the Halakhah cited previously, there is another reference to Beruriah in the Tosefta (Kelim B.M. 1:3): "Beruriah says that a door bolt may be drawn off one door and hung on another on the Sabbath" (without violating the stricture against work on the Sabbath). When this law was repeated before Rabbi Joshua, he said, "Beruriah ruled correctly." This law was also incorporated into the Mishnah (Kelim 11:4) under Rabbi Joshua's name.

In Biblical exegesis, Beruriah is credited with the guiding principle and exegetical rule of "look to the end of the verse." This is expounded in two instances in the Talmud (Berakoth 10a). In one case it is related that a sectary (non-believer) said to Beruriah, "It is written (Isaiah 54:1) 'Sing, O barren, thou that didst not hear.' Because she did not have children is she to sing?" Beruriah replied, "You fool! Look at the end of the verse where it is written, 'For the children of the desolate shall be more than the children of the married wife, saith the Lord.' The point being that at present she is barren but in the future, as related by the end of the passage, she shall have many children." Another point made by Beruriah was that by "the desolate," Isaiah means Jerusalem and the "married wife" is a simile for Rome, so that in the future Judea and Jerusalem would be more numerous than Rome. Ending the story with a sharp retort, Beruriah concluded, "But what then is the meaning of 'a barren woman that did not bear'? Sing, O community of Israel who resembles a barren woman for not having born children like you for Gehenna."

Beruriah's womanly tenderness as well as her skill in Biblical exegesis is illustrated by the following story in connection with her husband Rabbi Meir, the most brilliant of the younger generation of Tannaim and Rabbi Akiba's prize student. The Talmud (Ber. 10a) relates that there were once highwaymen in the neighborhood where Rabbi Meir lived who caused him a great deal of trouble. Rabbi Meir prayed that they should die. Hearing him, his wife Beruriah asked what legal authority he had for such a prayer? "Is it because the Psalmist (Ps. 104:35) says, 'Let *hatta'im* cease out of the earth.' Is it written *hot'im* (sinners)? It is written *hatta'im* (sins). Furthermore, look at the end of the verse: 'and let the wicked be no more.' Since sins will cease, there will be no more wicked men. Rather pray that they should repent and they will be no more wicked." He did pray and they repented.

Beruriah guided many students in their studies. She once discovered a student who was studying in an undertone (Erubin 53b-54a). Rebuking him, she exclaimed, "Is it not written, 'Ordered in all things, and sure' (II Samuels 23:25). If the Torah be ordered in the 248 organs of your body, including the organs of speech, it will be sure, and if not it will not be sure.'

Her ready wit often contained an undertone of resentment concerning the discrimination against women. Rabbi Jose the Galilean was once on a journey when he met Beruriah (Erubin 53b). "By what road," he asked her, "do we go to Lydda?"

"Foolish Galilean," she gibed, "did not the Sages say engage not in much talk with women? You should have asked: How to Lydda?"

The story by which Beruriah is best known is the one that shows her strength of character and total commitment to the will of the Almighty. It concerns the tragic death of her two sons on the Sabbath which occurred while their father was at the house of study (Yalkut, Prov. 964). When he returned at the conclusion of the Sabbath, Rabbi Meir asked for his sons. Beruriah told him they had gone to the house of study. Disregarding her husband's reply that he had already looked for them there, she handed him the cup of wine for the Habdalah service. His second inquiry for them was evaded by the answer that they had just gone out for a moment and would soon return. She proceeded to serve Rabbi Meir his evening meal. After he had eaten, Beruriah asked formally for permission to put a halakhic question to him.

"Rabbi," she began, "some time ago a deposit was left with me for safekeeping, and now the owner has come to claim it. Must I return it?"

"Can there be any question about the return of property to its owner?" answered Rabbi Meir, astonished that his wife should entertain a doubt. "I did not care to let it go out of my possession without your knowledge," replied Beruriah, and, taking him by the hand, led him into the room in which the bodies of their two sons lay on the bed.

When she drew back the cover, Rabbi Meir broke into tears and plaints over his two brilliant sons. Gently, Beruriah reminded him of his answer to her question about the return of a treasure entrusted to one for safekeeping, adding the verse from Job (1:21), "The Lord gave and the Lord hath taken away; blessed be the name of the Lord."

Tragedy again struck Beruriah, from another direction. Her father, Rabbi Hananiah ben Teradion, was arrested by the Romans for teaching the Torah. Condemned to die by torture, he was wrapped in the scroll of the Torah and placed on a pyre of green brush. The brush was set afire and wet wool was placed on his chest to prolong his agonies before dying. As further punishment, his wife was cruelly put to death and his youngest daughter was consigned to a government house of shame in Rome. It is interesting to note that Beruriah was not harmed, probably because she was married to Rabbi Meir, a noted apolitical individual and close friend of Acher, an infamous Roman adherent, spy, and Jewish traitor.

Beruriah implored her husband to do something to save her sister. Rabbi Meir himself set out to rescue her. Disguised as a knight he gained entrance to the brothel, bribed the jailer, and escaped with his charge. Soon after, however, the matter became known to the government and the warder, after being tortured, finally confessed what had happened. Drawings of Rabbi Meir's likeness were distributed throughout the Roman Empire and he was traced to Palestine. To avoid capture, Rabbi Meir escaped to Babylonia where he remained until the death of Hadrian. Here the Talmud (Aboda Zarah 18a) adds an enigmatic phrase that has puzzled scholars and fired the imagination of writers. "Some say it was because of that incident (the story just related) that he ran away to Babylonia; others say because of the incident about Beruriah." What incident is never discussed, mentioned, or alluded to in the Talmud or in the Midrash. Rashi quotes a degrading story that was prevalent in the Middle Ages. "Once Beruriah scoffed at the Rabbinical saying, 'Women are light-headed' (Kiddushin

80b), and ner husband warned her that her own end might yet testify to the truth of the words. To put her virtue to the test, he charged one of his disciples to endeavor to seduce her. After repeated efforts she yielded, and then shame drove her to commit suicide. Rabbi Meir, tortured by remorse, fled from his home."

This story is wholly at variance with what is known of Beruriah's character and that of Rabbi Meir. It is almost inconceivable that Beruriah would engage in such an immoral act and even more unbelievable that Rabbi Meir would actively engage his own student to seduce a married woman, a cardinal sin for both. A more plausible explanation of the passage in question is that Beruriah, who was noted for her sharp wit and incisive verbal barbs, not always under firm control, said something against the Roman occupiers so that Rabbi Meir was forced to seek refuge in Babylonia. Since no mention is made of Beruriah after this incident, it is presumed that she must have died about this time.

The final events of Beruriah's life are lost in history. What we do know, however, is that she was superior to most of the Tannaim or rabbinic scholars of her age, proof that sex is not a determining factor as far as knowledge of Talmud or Halakhah is concerned.

Dona Gracia

In November of 1491, Granada, the last seat of Mohamme-
dan power in Spain, surrendered to Ferdinand and
Isabella, the Catholic sovereigns of Spain. All of Spain was
now united politically and religiously, yet there remained
one discordant group, the Jews. While the final battle for
Granada was still raging, the king and queen had begun to
consider ridding the country of its Jewish population in
order to make Spain completely homogeneous. Accordingly, on March 30, 1492, an edict was issued by the terms
of which not a single Jew was to exist in Spain by July 30.
Any Jew who remained after that date was to be put to
death unless he submitted to baptism.

Nothing could make the royal pair change their minds.
A few Jews converted; some became Marranos, that is, outwardly Christians but secretly Jews, and the rest, about
200,000, left for various parts of the world. The fortunate
ones made their way to Turkey where they were received
warmly by the ruling Sultan. The Sultan marveled at the
folly of the Spanish monarchs who had impoverished their
own country and enriched his. Many Jews were captured
on the high seas by pirates and sold as slaves. Many were
sold as slaves by the captains of the ships hired to take
them to a safe haven. Others died from various epidemics
and diseases, due to rotten food and inadequate shelter,

while they were awaiting transportation to safety. Many, having survived their journey became fatally ill in temporary camps.

A few of the wealthiest families and a number of highly skilled craftsmen, especially those engaged in the manufacture of munitions, were allowed to settle in Portugal. In 1497, however, the King of Portugal, Manoel I, contracted to marry the daughter of Ferdinand and Isabella and ordered all the Jews out of his kingdom by October of that same year. The king was nonetheless loath to see so many of his richest and most influential citizens leave. Against church policy, he therefore forcibly baptized the Jews of his kingdom. While some managed to escape soon after, the majority continued to live in Portugal secretly as Jews. King Manoel moreover had pledged his word that for 20 (some say for 29) years, Jews would not be molested by the dreaded Inquisition, the instrument whereby the Catholic Church could investigate Catholics suspected of relapses into either Judaism or any other heresy. The penalty, upon conviction, was anything the inquisitors decided, including burning at the stake and confiscation of all wealth. The Inquisition was directed almost entirely against the New Christians and Marranos. It became the most barbarous, degrading, and corrupt institution of the Catholic Church. As a result of the king's promise, the Portuguese Marranos followed Jewish observances with less secrecy than those in Spain and were able to offer more religious instruction of the young in the Bible and other Jewish literature.

The Inquisition was finally introduced into Portugal in 1531. It was stopped soon after, then reintroduced. There were obstacles to its proper functioning which continued until 1539. From then on, however, it became progressively more severe and exacting, eventually equalling the worst horrors of the Spanish Inquisition.

In these brutal times, there lived a remarkable woman, blessed with intelligence, grace, character, and foresight, a brilliant businesswoman and a great philanthropist with intense loyalty to Judaism. She was born in Portugal (c. 1510), the daughter of Marrano parents, and named Beatrice (later she changed her name to Gracia) de Luna. Her family bore the illustrious Jewish name of Nasi. They instilled in her an abiding commitment to her Jewish heritage. Throughout her life, Gracia's most fervent desire was to practice openly the religion she loved.

In 1528 Gracia married Francisco Mendes, a Marrano of similar background and belief. Francisco and his brother Diogo, who had married Gracia's sister Reyna, were important dealers in precious stones and spices. They later expanded into banking and established branches all over Europe, one of the most important of which was in Antwerp. While Francisco remained in Lisbon, his brother Diogo went to head the branch in Antwerp. With the imposition of the Inquisition in Portugal, the Antwerp branch soon surpassed the main Lisbon office in importance. This was not by accident or due to economic conditions, but was rather by design of the Mendes's. Under the rules of the Inquisition, anyone convicted of harboring Jewish beliefs, lost not only his life but his fortune as well. It was obviously more practical for the Inquisition to try rich heretics than poor ones, and it soon became imperative for the Mendes family to leave Portugal. However, there were two major obstacles. The business had to be relocated, and the family had to contrive to obtain government permission to leave, a seemingly impossible task.

In 1535, before either of these objectives could be accomplished, Francisco Mendes died, leaving Gracia a young widow of 26. Within two years, Gracia, unknown of course to the authorities, accomplished the task of transferring almost all her assets to Antwerp. She then set out on her second objective, to leave Portugal with her only daughter Reyna and her nephew Joao Miquez who had come to live with her after his father's death. She set sail with her entire family for England. Evidently the authorities were given sound financial reasons for her going to England, Since this was not the usual way of escaping the Inquisition, the Portuguese government saw no reason to refuse her permission. In addition, to allay any suspicions, Gracia left her house and estates as if the family intended to return. From England, however, she sailed for Antwerp and there joined her brother-in-law in 1537.

In addition to assuming an active and equal role in the vast family business, Gracia began her lifelong philanthropic career. She wholeheartedly joined her brother-in-law in attempts to convince the Pope to stop the Inquisition in Portugal. These efforts, only initially successful, were directed toward changing papal policy by bribing emissaries and other important functionaries of the Roman Catholic Church. Her generosity also enabled poor Marranos to flee the ravages of the Inquisition. Still unhappy, although accepted socially by the aristocracy, Gracia longed to throw off her Christian mask and practice her religion freely.

Gracia importuned her brother-in-law, Diogo, to either reestablish the business elsewhere, in a place where she could declare herself a Jewess, or pay over her share of the property and allow her to go. Diogo and Gracia came to some understanding, but before their plans could be implemented, he died. According to his will, she was left sole administrator of the huge business and trustee of his wife's and daughter's fortune.

Other problems now presented themselves. The king of France cast a covetous eye on the fortune of the house of Mendes. An accusation was made by the imperial court that the deceased Diogo Mendes had secretly practiced Judaism. It was therefore decreed that the whole of his estate in France, being that of a heretic, should be forfeited to the crown. Gracia somehow succeeded in averting this calamity by a few handsome and judicious bribes to powerful officials and a huge loan to the king. It was now, however, impossible for her to leave without exciting the government's suspicions against herself and endangering her property and her fortune. In addition, several Christian noblemen had asked for the hand of her daughter Reyna. It was becoming increasingly difficult to find legitimate excuses for her refusal of so many illustrious suitors.

Within two years, Gracia was again able to resolve all her difficulties. A story was circulated by her agents that her nephew Joao Miquez had fled to Venice with her daughter Reyna. This afforded her and the family a pretext for their journey to Venice. Again she was able to transfer most of her fortune, this time from Antwerp, which was under the aegis of the Spanish king. As before, the household and various estates continued to function as if her immediate return was expected. No one offered any obstacles and in 1547 she and her entire family arrived in Venice. Charles V, hearing of her successful ruse, in fury seized whatever he could lay his hands on, which was still a considerable amount of property.

It was in Venice, where safety was assured, that disaster struck from an unsuspected corner. Her sister Reyna, reckless, silly, and lacking in common sense, demanded her own and her daughter's share of the estate to do with as she pleased. As this would have been detrimental to the functioning of the business and Gracia had been appointed by Diogo to be guardian of his minor daughter and trustee of her property until her marriage, Gracia refused. The younger sister, anxious to escape Gracia's guardianship, took a step, incredibly foolish, that redounded to her own misfortune. She informed the Venetian government that Dona Gracia was about to emigrate to Turkey, taking with her all her wealth, and that she there intended to openly resume her adherence to Judaism. On the other hand, Reyna assured the authorities that she and her daughter desired to remain Christians. An appeal was presented to Venetian authorities to assist her in obtaining possession of her property in order to use it as a good Christian. Seeing a magnificent prize at hand, the rulers of Venice took up the accusation, cited Gracia to appear before the authorities, and arrested her to prevent flight. Reyna also sent a messenger to France to denounce Gracia as a Jewess and to take over the considerable property she had there in her name. The messenger, a vicious antisemite, denounced both sisters as Jewesses to the King of France who immediately confiscated their huge estates in addition to cancelling his own large debt to the family.

Gracia was helped by her nephew Joao and the Sultan's physician, Moses Hamon, formerly a Spanish Marrano. They induced Sultan Solyman of Turkey to embrace her cause by pointing out to him that immense riches were about to be brought into his dominions and the Venetian republic had deprived him of them. A special messenger of state was sent by the Sublime Porte, ruler of Turkey, to Venice with instructions that Gracia was to be set free at once and allowed to depart for Turkey with all her property. She was freed promptly but negotiations for the release of her property dragged on for several years.

While awaiting resolution of these affairs, Gracia found a haven in Ferrara under the liberal-minded Duke. There for the first time in her life she was able to throw off the disguise of Christianity and openly espouse Judaism. It was there that she assumed her Jewish name of Gracia (Hannah) Nasi.

In Ferrara, she continued the noble work of organizing the flight of hundreds of fugitive Marranos and operating an underground railroad from Portugal. The poet Samuel

Usque describes her achievements in the most glowing terms. "The Lord hath. . .united every virtue in one person. . .in the lovely form of the blessed Jewess Nasi. She it was who, at the beginning of the dispersion (of the Marranos), gave strength and hope to the perishing sons, made hopeless by their want of means to escape the fire, and encouraged them to go forth on their pilgrimage. With bountiful hand did she succor those who had already set out on their wanderings in Flanders and other parts, and who, weakened by poverty and overcome by the perils of the sea passage, were in danger of getting no further, and strengthened them in their need. . .With her pure hand and her heavenly will had she freed most of this nation (of Marranos) from the depths of endless misery, poverty, and sin, led them into safe places, and gathered them together into obedience to the precepts of the true God."

The renowned Ferrara Bible, published in 1533 by two Marranos, was dedicated to Gracia Nasi. This work, later reprinted in various cities during the sixteenth and seventeenth centuries, sustained many Marranos who wished to return to their true faith but understood only Spanish. The dedication of this celebrated book reads as follows: "We desire to dedicate the translation to your grace, as the person whose desserts among our people will always occupy the foremost place. May you be pleased to accept it, to favor and protect it with the spirit which has always favored those who have asked help of you."

Many noted rabbis of the time were equally lavish in praise of Dona Gracia Nasi. "The noble princess, the glory of Israel, the wise woman who builds her house in holiness and purity, with her hands sustains the poor and needy, in order to make them happy in this world, and blessed in the world to come. Many are they whom she has rescued from death, and lifted up from the abasement of a worthless life, when they were languishing in a dungeon, and were given over to death. She hath founded houses wherein all may learn the law of God. She has given to many whereby they may not only live, but live in plenty."

Unwilling to harbor a grudge, Gracia became reconciled with her sister, married off her sister's daughter to her nephew Samuel, and provided generously for the young couple. In 1553 she settled, with her daughter Reyna, in Constantinople where her activities on behalf of her fellow Jews were expanded. The poor and needy received generous assistance, houses of prayer and schools were established, and scholars and teachers of Talmud were encouraged. One particular synagogue in Constantinople bore her name and was extant until a few years ago.

While they were in Constantinople, Reyna married her gifted cousin Joao Miquez, but not before he made an open avowal of Judaism and assumed his Jewish name of Joseph Nasi. After that Joseph Nasi later to become the Duke of Naxos became associated with Dona Gracia in all of her in numerable enterprises, both political and commercial. These businesses ranged from shipping, banking and trading to selling materials and holding various concessions, including the valuable and most important wine monopoly. A brilliant entrepreneur wherever she ventured money came easily to her.

In 1556-67, Dona Gracia attempted something really astonishing, coming when it did and considering against whom it was directed. Pope Paul IV, one of the more vicious antisemitic Popes to sit on the throne of Saint Peter, imprisoned the Marranos of Ancona and eventually burned 26 of them at the stake. This affected Dona Gracia deeply. In an attempt to punish the Pope for this inhuman deed, she organized a boycott of the papal port of Ancona. The Jewish merchants of Turkey controlled a considerable portion of world trade and they used Ancona as the principal port of entry for wares shipped from Turkey to Europe. Trade was to be transferred to the port of Pesaro, thereby ruining the port of Ancona and cutting off a vital source of revenue for the Pope. To succeed, however, the plan needed the full cooperation of every Jewish merchant in Turkey or, failing that, every rabbi. This proved an impossible task even for Dona Gracia, for most people were not as farsighted as she. Moreover, the Pope did not sit idle. He threatened the Jews of Italy with expulsion should they go along with the scheme. He also accused the Duke of Pesaro of heresy and threatened him with excommunication. To protect himself, the Duke had to ask all the Marranos to leave and the whole plan fell apart. However, had the Jewish merchants and rabbis acted immediately, with conviction and decisiveness, the Duke of Pesaro, with huge revenues coming his way, might have stood up to the Pope. The Pope and other powerful antisemites would have realized that they could not oppress Jews as long as the Jews had resources. The Jews' lot would have been improved and hundreds if not thousands of Jews and Marranos would have been saved. Gracia understood this, but it was beyond the imagination of others. Encouraged by the timidity of his opponents, the Pope continued to hound and kill Marranos, burning the Talmud and other Hebrew books. He was instrumental in the expulsion of numerous Jews from their homes and countries throughout various parts of Europe.

For the remaining years of her life, Dona Gracia was occupied with another great vision, the resettlement of Palestine. She intuitively realized that Palestine, even at that time, was the only sanctuary for persecuted Jewry. In the years following the expulsion of the Jews from Spain, Palestine had become more widely settled than at any other time since the Crusades. Spanish Jews with technical skills developed small businesses; rabbis came and established centers of Rabbinic learning; mystics and students of the Cabbala organized their great center at Safed, making Safed the most important city of Palestine. The Jewish community in Jerusalem was enlarged. Dona Gracia decided to create a settlement in the desolate and unpopulated city of Tiberias.

Why choose Tiberias as the starting point of what was to be a Jewish homeland? To have picked Jerusalem, the ancient capital, would have aroused fears and suspicion among the Arab population and Turkish rulers. Safed, already populated with a considerable number of Jews could have been a likely starting point except that its inhabitants were almost entirely immersed in mystical studies and exercises. These were not the most likely people to be interested in the practical work of building a state. Tiberias, with its splendid site, fertile surroundings, and great historical memories was as good as and perhaps better than any other site. In addition, some rabbis may have told Gracia of a Talmudic statement claiming that the redemption was to start from Tiberias. However, most important to her ideas, Tiberias was suitable for agriculture and industries based on agricultural products.

About 1558, the Sultan leased to Gracia the city of Tiberias and some seven neighboring villages for the sum of 1,000 ducats yearly. It was to be a refuge for the Jews of the world who were being mercilessly persecuted everywhere except in Turkey and its dominions. Before people were willing to settle there, a wall had to be constructed as protection against sudden attack from roving bands of marauders. Completed in the winter of 1564-65, the wall's total perimeter was a modest 1,500 yards. People came, appropriated deserted houses, restored them, cleared ruins, and revived the city. An ancient synagogue was reopened at the lakeside, abutting on the wall. Dona Gracia constructed a mansion for her private use outside the city walls near the famous hot baths which were still frequented by visitors. Her intention was to settle there with her entire retinue in 1566; whether she did or not was never recorded. However, her absence from Constantinople from the year 1566 until her death, leads one to suspect that she achieved her ambition.

Realizing that it would be impossible to build the nucleus of a sound and healthy Jewish community on the mysticism of Safed or the petty trade of the other small cities of Palestine, Dona Gracia now endeavored to establish her tiny principality on a sound economic basis. It was necessary to have an agricultural base with strong roots in the soil, as well as handicrafts, manufacturing, and trade developing from this base with which the Jews of the Mediterranean were closely associated. The industry that had all these qualifications was silk production and manufacturing. It could provide a livelihood for a large number of persons at every stage. The first step was to obtain the raw material. Mulberry trees were planted for the silkworms which, together with the other agricultural products of the area and fish from the lake, enabled many Jewish refugees to find food, a pleasant climate, and industry awaiting their arrival.

Soon results were apparent. By 1554 the city had become a veritable garden of Eden, with date palms, orange groves, pine trees, vineyards, and household gardens. Dona Gracia did not neglect food for the soul either. By 1562 the talmudic academy in Tiberias, supported almost exclusively by her, nearly rivaled that of Safed.

Upon Dona Gracia's death in 1569 the ideological force behind the project waned because the Duke of Naxos, her nephew and son-in-law, had far more extensive and ambitious plans than a tiny Jewish principality. The foresight and vision which she possessed could not be infused into him. First to disappear was the academy with whose activities he was not in sympathy. An outbreak of violence in 1575 caused most of the wealthier inhabitants to leave. In 1579, Bedouins and other Arabs attacked, thus reducing the population still further. Moreover, Jewish immigration to Palestine was not very extensive or popular. The rabbis were still convinced that redemption would begin only with the coming of the Messiah. Thus, the Tiberias experiment did not live up to the hopes of its founder. It was not until 1740 when Rabbi Hayim Abulaffia settled in Tiberias with a number of Jews, rebuilt the city and planted vineyards and olive groves that the city became a permanent Jewish settlement.

Dona Gracia was an illustrious woman of lavish generosity and sublime vision. As a young widow she took over a huge and complex business, ran it successfully and was able to rescue most of her fortune before calamity struck not once but thrice. She saved hundreds of Marranos from persecution and death. With brilliant strategy she tried to punish Jewish murderers and antisemites by imposing an economic boycott which unfortunately for the Jews, proved, like many of her projects, to be in advance of its time. Gracia's greatest vision and insight was for a Jewish homeland in Palestine, a place where Jews would become the majority, and eventually achieve selfgovernment backed by a viable economy, and based on agriculture, manufacturing, and exportation.

While most historians have generally recognized Dona Gracia as noteworthy, they favor her nephew and son-in-law, the flamboyant and seemingly more worldly Duke of Naxos. A careful reading of history, however, shows that when Dona Gracia's guiding hand was no longer present, the fortunes of the Duke of Naxos, although retaining some momentum because of the law of inertia, eventually declined.

There was no living issue from the marriage of Dona Gracia's daughter Reyna and the Duke of Naxos. The fortune she had amassed was gradually dissipated by her son-in-law. The Tiberias experiment ultimately failed. History has not been kind to this munificent woman.

Glueckel of Hameln

Glueckel of Hameln, who is the most famous Jewess of the late seventeenth and early eighteenth centures, was born in 1647 or 1648 and died in 1724 at the age of 78. An energetic woman of strong character, Glueckel was able to surmount tragedy and innumerable hardships. She wrote of her family and community in a natural and vivid style which is unique for the light it sheds on the period and the difficult hand-to-mouth existence of the Jews of the time.

Glueckel began her memoir (consisting of seven short books) in 1690, shortly after the death of her husband, when she was about 45 years old. A gifted natural writer, who had time on her hands throughout interminable sleepless nights, Glueckel wrote of her childhood and marriage. The language she used was Judaeo-German, written in Hebrew letters. This language, mainly German with Hebrew comprising approximately 15 percent of the total vocabulary, is the precursor of modern Yiddish. The book was first published in 1896 by Dr. David Kaufman who transcribed it into German from the copy that Glueckel's son Moses, Rabbi of Baiersdorf, had made from the original manuscript. It was recognized almost immediately as both a classic as well as a rich historical, sociological, and philological source and it has been further translated into several languages.

Glueckel was born in Hamburg, Germany, the daughter of Beila and Leib Pinkerle. When she was three years old, the Jews were driven from Hamburg. They sought refuge in Altona, a village 15 minutes journey away, which was then under the more benevolent rule of the King of Denmark. Glueckel's father was the second richest Jew in Altona, worth 8,000 reichsthalers, a capital representing about eight years of moderate livelihood. Her maternal grandmother lived with the family. Glueckel used to listen avidly to her grandmother's tales of life during the Thirty Years' War and the epidemics that accompanied it. Her grandmother described how most of her family and all of her fortune were destroyed; how she and her daughter, Glueckel's mother, earned their living making fine lace using silver and gold thread, and how they earned money teaching young girls the trade.

The Thirty Years' War had ended in 1648, leaving Germany destitute and in chaos. Men burned witches and endeavored to transmute lead into gold with equal hysteria. Since the Middle Ages, the Jews of Central Europe had sunk very low in the economic scale and their means of subsistence was precarious and severely restricted. The guilds were closed to them, while the Fuggers and their imitators had taken over the Jews' banking and other mercantile activities. The end of the Thirty Years' War and the financial depression of the second half of the seventeenth century gave the Jews an opportunity to better themselves.

The Jews, including Glueckel's father, were given permission to return to Hamburg. It was, however, with the understanding that the town council could compel them to leave at any time and that they were not to be allowed to attend a public synagogue.

At a time when most people were uneducated, Glueckel attended school and was taught not only to pray, but to read and write as well. Her aptitude for her studies is borne out by her narrative, which is laced with stories and excerpts from morality and pietistic works. In accordance with the customs prevailing at that time Glueckel was betrothed at the age of 12 to Chaim Goldschmidt, aged 13, of Hameln (Hamelin, the town of Pied Piper fame). The betrothal was accompanied by a contract, a carefully written business agreement whereby the parents give the young couple a dowry and stipulate the length of time they were prepared to support their children (*kest*), thus enabling the young people to marry, start their own family, and acquire the knowledge, skills and abilities for earning a livelihood.

After a betrothal lasting two years, Glueckel set off with her parents to meet and marry her future husband. Her unbounded zest and happy disposition, enabled her to adapt rapidly to her newly acquired family in Hameln, a dreary little village compared to Hamburg, with only two resident Jewish families. Chaim, who disliked the town in which he was born and raised, was impatient to leave. He felt that business opportunities were more favorable in Hamburg. Nevertheless, the young couple sought permission from his parents before they moved to Hamburg, where they lived with Glueckel's parents for two years.

Chaim went into the business of buying up old gold and selling it to jewelers and merchants. Glueckel, who had become pregnant on her return to Hamburg, gave birth to a daughter at the same time as her mother and tells an amusing story of a mix-up. The two women shared a small room together after the birth of their daughters, where they were visited by all their friends and neighbors who came to gawk at mother and daughter in childbed together, an unusual occasion even in those times. Glueckel returned to her own room in order to ease their discomfort and congestion. As she was very young and this was her first child, her mother insisted that the baby remain where she was, and promised that the maid would bring it to her at feeding time. This arrangement suited Glueckel and gave her a good night's sleep except for the midnight feeding. One night she awoke suddenly and with dread realized that the maid had not brought her baby. Frantically she ran to her mother's room and with difficulty roused the maid, demanding to know where her baby was. The commotion awakened her mother who also wanted to know what had happened to the child. When Glueckel suggested that the baby nestling beside her mother in bed might be her own, her mother clutched the baby tightly, refusing to part with it. Glueckel took her mother by the hand and led her over to the cradle where the other baby lay peacefully asleep, oblivious of the commotion surrounding it. The whole household had awakened in alarm which quickly turned to laughter when the mystery was finally unraveled.

Chaim Hameln's (taking the name of the town was common then) business prospered. He travelled to Danzig and Amsterdam buying goods at import or manufacturing centers and selling them at the German trade fairs, especially the larger ones in Frankfurt and Leipzig. There were contracts for delivering silver to the governmental mints and discounting bills of exchange. While Chaim was away, Glueckel looked after the business at home, in addition to taking care of her household and numerous children. Trusted and respected by her beloved husband, Glueckel was consulted before Chaim entered into any business agreement and even drew up these partnership agreements after a while. They were able to post agents, usually relatives, in Denmark and Holland. One of them, Judah Berlin (born Jost Liebman), later became court factor (banker) to Frederick I of Prussia, and the richest Jew in all of eastern Europe.

Chaim was not a robust man and was frequently ill. His health was not improved by attending the various fairs. This situation was not aided by the fact that Jews were given the least desirable fair areas, such as Leipzig, where the

Jewish section was situated in a stinking swamp. In addition to Chaim's physical weakness, he underwent an additional mental stress, because if a Jew died at a fair, all his goods and money were forfeit. One had to be careful where to die. Glueckel described how, with influence and large sums of money, the body of Mendel Speyer of Frankfurt was removed for burial to Dessau, the closest Jewish community, 30 miles from Leipzig. Chaim himself became very ill on one of his business trips to Halberstadt and was unable to return home in time for the festival of Shavuoth. He was brought home after the festival by friends who took turns traveling by his side and ministering to his needs.

Life was hazardous. The handicaps under which the Jews lived were enormous; they were safe nowhere. A Jew had to pay money for his travel documents, was subject to a body tax every time he entered the large towns, and was not permitted to own property. He not only paid duty on his merchandise, but he himself was considered no better than "chalk, cheese, charcoal . . .", as Glueckel wrote in her diary. Even the lucrative and important position of court factor to the princes of the various principalities was extremely precarious. Wealth could disappear overnight, and the factor faced jail and hanging if his protector was vindictive.

In contrast to her husband, Glueckel enjoyed excellent health. She bore 13 children, only one of whom died in childhood. This was a rare feat for the time as the mortality rate was very high. In a matter-of-fact way, in the midst of bearing children, nursing them, and doing business, the Hamelns were also saving money for dowries in order to marry off the older children. Five of the 12 children married into the most prominent families of the day. Zipporah, the oldest daughter, a very attractive child, married Kosman, the son of Elias Cleve (born Elijah Gompertz), financial agent of the Great Elector. The sumptuous wedding, held in Elias

Cleve's palatial mansion, took place in the presence of Prince Friedrich, heir to the Elector of Brandenburg, and Prince Maurice of Nassau, who happened to be visiting Cleve at the time of the wedding and had informed the court factor of his desire to attend.

Zipporah, the bride, received a dowry of 2,000 reichsthalers from her parents, in addition to which 100 reichsthalers were given toward the cost of the wedding. A reception was held before the wedding ceremony at which various foods, wines and fruits were served. It was customary to produce and count the dowry at the reception, but with so many guests present there was no time. In the general excitement nobody had given any thought to the marriage contract (*ketubah*) which, after a hasty consultation by the rabbis present, had to be written out immediately after the marriage had taken place instead of before as it should have been. Subsequently the guests were led into a fine spacious hall, in the center of which stood a long table loaded with delicacies. There they were served in strict order of precedence. The table was removed after all the guests had eaten at which time everybody was entertained with various short masques ending with the immensely popular Totentanse (Dance of Death). This Dance of Death was a popular form of entertainment in seventeenth century Europe. It portrayed the ultimate triumph of death usually depicted as a skeleton leading live persons or other skeletons to the grave.

Throughout Glueckel's books are vivid anecdotes which describe the social, economic, and precarious life of the Jews of her time. Wedding feasts were not only occasions for rejoicing, but opportunities for arranging marriages and business matters and for advancing oneself by courting powerful princes.

Among the guests at Zipporah's wedding was a Portuguese jeweler bearing the famous Sephardic name of

Mocatta. He wore an exquisite gold watch set with diamonds which Elias Cleve wished to purchase and present as a gift to Prince Friedrich. Cleve was dissuaded, however, by a friend who suggested that although it might be worthwhile if he was the Elector of Brandenburg himself, it certainly was not wise giving such an expensive present to a mere princeling of 13 years. The young man became Elector several months later and Elias Cleve ever after recalled the incident with anger and regret, always berating his ex-friend whenever they met.

As to Glueckel's other children: Moses was married to the daughter of Simson Baiersdorf, court factor to the duchy of Kalmbach-Bayreuth; Samuel to the niece of Samson Wertheimer, court Jew to the Emperor Leopold I; Esther to the son of Moses Krumbach, a leading financier of Lorraine; Freudchen to Mordecai Hamburger, who later moved to London, founded his own synagogue, and then went to India where he made a fortune; Nathan almost married the daughter of Samuel Oppenheimer, court factor in Vienna, but became his agent instead and married a girl from another substantial family. The others all made respectable matches.

Glueckel frequently touches upon the subject of dowries. In her father's generation, 300 or 400 reichsthalers was commonplace. As mentioned, Zipporah, her eldest daughter, was dowered with 2,000 reichsthalers, Mordecai received 3,000 and Nathan 4,000. At the turn of the century dowries of 15,000 to 30,000 reichsthalers are mentioned. It was a vital necessity, especially for a young adolescent couple, in order to start a family and establish a business. It is interesting to note here that dowries were given to all children, not only the girls, and that the costs of the wedding, large elaborate affairs with as many as 400 guests present, were borne by the parents of both bride and groom.

In her memoirs Glueckel discussed her feelings during her numerous pregnancies, at the birth of her children, and during important events. There are references to the circumcision of her sons, the weddings of her children, *shiva* (seven days of mourning) for her husband, although nowhere is there the slightest hint or suggestion of a Bar Mitzvah. There was obviously no ceremony or party to celebrate the event probably because the children were betrothed at this age. Religious observance was so natural a part of her life that there is little need for discussion of it in her book. Religious events, however, are described in detail.

Glueckel had no illusions about poverty—she lived too close to it for comfort, in spite of being considered a woman of substantial means. Business was precarious; one year was excellent, the next could result in deficits that erased the wealth acquired in previous years. In 1689, when Glueckel was 44 years old, her husband of 30 years died, leaving her to cope alone with the business, large debts and six children to dower and marry off. She had no one to turn to because most people had difficulty coping with their own problems. After the period of mourning, she sold off all her merchandise to clear her husband's debts and maintain his unblemished reputation. With the remainder of the money from the sale she started afresh, buying and selling seed pearls. Alone, with very little help, she ran the business, traveleled to the numerous fairs, bought and sold merchandise, managed a stocking factory, and married off her children with substantial dowries and suitable weddings. People liked and respected her even though in negotiating the dowries and in her business dealings she drove a hard bargain.

When Glueckel arrived in Bamberg after the betrothal of her son Samuel to the daughter of Moses Bamberg, brother-in-law of Rabbi Samson Wertheimer, court factor to the Emperor in Vienna, she was informed that instead of a dowry of 4,000 reichsthalers, the wedding would not take place without another 1,000 reichsthalers. Glueckel refused, preferring to await the letter from Samson Wertheimer which would prove that the amount deposited was the figure agreed upon. She was correct, the wedding finally took place, and there she discussed a match for her son Moses. Immediately after Samuel's wedding, she journeyed to Furth to meet the girl selected for Moses and her parents. However, they were not there. Anxious to conclude the betrothal agreement and sensing her anxiety to return home, the marriage broker chased after her and begged her to remain a while. Informing Glueckel that the sons of Baiersdorf had arrived with authority to agree to terms, he managed to persuade her to spend the night at a small inn a short ride from Bamberg. The betrothal agreement was duly signed, Glueckel then traveled to Bayreuth to meet the father, who was forced to remain there due to urgent business. The wedding was delayed over a year because Samson Baiersdorf, court factor to the duchy of Kalmbach-Bayreuth, was having difficulty maintaining his position.

Immediately after Moses's wedding, Glueckel, 10 years a widow, married again. Aged 54, having resisted many excellent matches over the years, she now longed for security. The strain of attending fairs winter and summer, the dread of failure, bankruptcy, and loss of her reputation, and the fear of becoming dependent on and a burden to her children were becoming too much for her to bear.

A match was suggested by her son-in-law, Moses Krumbach of Metz. Her implicit confidence in his judgment led her to agree to marry the president of the community in Metz, Reb Hirsch Levy, whose excellent reputation in business would, she thought, not only be of benefit to herself but to her children as well. Her reliance was misplaced: within a year after the marriage had taken place, Hirsch Levy had lost all his money and most of hers and

Nathan's, her son who had invested with him. She was able to salvage her son's money but when Hersch Levy died 12 years later, only a third of the dowry she had brought into the marriage was returned to her. During those years they were supported by his children, and much as she regretted her actions, no time was wasted in useless recriminations. Her own financial experiences made her recognize that the bankruptcy was due to business and economic factors beyond his control.

After his death, Glueckel's children begged her to move into their home, but they were always rebuffed. She preferred to live alone even though the severe cold and the climb to her tiny room in an attic proved too exhausting for her and she had to spend her days and nights in front of the fire in her landlord's kitchen. Finally, after a particularly severe illness during one long winter, she was forced to move in with her daughter.

Glueckel's daughter Esther and her husband Moses had just moved into a magnificent new home. They gave her a room to herself, and she came and went as she pleased. Nothing but the finest food was served to her. The table was set, awaiting her even if she was late for the main meal of the day when the family dined together. Glueckel lived about nine years with Esther, whose generosity and hospitality to her mother and to all her guests, regardless of wealth, was a source of pride to Glueckel. She died in 1724, aged 76, six years after she had completed her last book.

Glueckel's sparkle, humor, and intelligence aided her considerably when money was scarce, and also contributed to the enchantment of her first marriage; the mutual respect, love and admiration, and discussion before decisions were taken all gave the marriage a thoroughly modern ring.

An extensive literature was available at this time in Judaeo-German. Not only religious works were translated but also secular, and some 385 titles are preserved in the Bodleian Library, Oxford, England. Glueckel alluded to and discussed many of these stories, homilies, and parables throughout her autobiography, a sure indication that she had read widely, in addition to the Bible which she quoted with confidence. Her natural gift as a writer and raconteuse must have contributed to the esteem in which she was held by all who knew her, including later generations who have become acquainted with her through her works.

Rahel Varnhagen

Toward the end of the eighteenth century there was a general spirit of scepticism and romanticism in Europe, especially in France, England, and Prussia. This was the age of Revolution, Enlightenment, and Emancipation. Greater personal liberty existed for women than had ever existed before and at the close of the eighteenth century women became intellectually self-conscious. This was the age of the salon, when women became leaders of cultural movements and their homes the rendezvous for the literary and intellectual lights of the day.

The salon, usually in a home, was the meeting place of people of various cultural, intellectual, and political backgrounds, where evenings were spent in the exchange of ideas. There were few alternative means of entertainment, and this was an inexpensive and delightful way of spending an evening. The hostess was usually intelligent and charming with a strong personality; otherwise she would never have been able to attract the people who gave the salon its aura of importance.

One of the outstanding figures of this period in Germany was Rabel Lewin Varnhagen, acclaimed as the greatest woman of her time and the greatest woman of all time. She was the center of artistic and literary Berlin. While these opinions are exaggerated, she was undeniably a powerful personality and never failed to leave an impression on those with whom she came into contact.

Born in Berlin in May or June of 1771, she was the daughter of a moderately wealthy jewel merchant, an observant Jew of great wit and intelligence who tyrannized his family. Rahel was the eldest of five children, three boys and two girls, all of whom were terrified by their father's violent temper. She suffered frequent illness during her childhood, and unpleasant situations, nervous excitement, and the weather caused her intense suffering. Her father tried to mold her in his own image, but she rebelled and ever after remembered her youth as one of constant anguish. Many years later she wrote, "no one ever had a more tormented youth than I had up to the age of 18 years." In self-defense she became reserved and spent many hours in an attic room, reading, thinking, and trying to expand her intellectual horizons by studying the works of Goethe which subsequently became the driving force of her existence.

Rahel's father died in 1789 or 1790, leaving very little money. Although her father's domineering presence no longer prevailed, she had to bear the full brunt of her mother's bitterness and frustrations. Throughout her mother's final illness in 1809, she nursed her devotedly. To Varnhagen in 1808 she wrote, "Yesterday I was meditating on human suffering and love and I thought the greatest passion loses its black magic, its death agonies if one has a mother, in the full sense of what that word can mean." After her mother's death, forced to rely on handouts from her brothers Markus and Moritz, she moved to a small house in Charlottenburg.

The years from 1790 to 1809 were important for the full development of Rahel's rich and understanding nature. Her younger brother Ludwig, "the brother of her heart," a budding author who moved in literary circles in Berlin, introduced her to his friends, all of whom she captivated.

Her attic room at home became their rendezvous and was the beginning of what was to become the greatest salon of nineteenth century Germany. David Veit, Fichte, Friedrich Gentz, and Prince Louis Ferdinand of Prussia all received encouragement, inspiration, and understanding from their tactful hostess. She possessed a beautiful clear voice, dark eyes, and intuitive understanding. Even people who had only met her once, paid tribute to her charm and the lasting influence she exerted. This garrett room, set apart from society as it was, attracted people from completely different social backgrounds who used it as a neutral meeting place.

Rahel's oldest and closest friend was David Veit, a Jew who later converted to Christianity. They corresponded, he with sympathy and understanding of her feelings and background, she withholding nothing, describing in detail her innermost thoughts and intense frustrations. This candor in her letters and journals was to remain throughout her life. She wrote frequently to all her acquaintances and kept all their letters to her. These letters and diaries form a nucleus describing the cultural life of Berlin at the time. Another friend with whom she corresponded was Henriette Herz, the wife of Marcus Herz, a physician and scientist. Together, Henriette and her husband established in their home the first Jewish salon. She was not nearly as brilliant or accomplished a letter writer as Rahel. Years later, after the death of her husband and mother, she too converted. The third well-known figure of the salon period was an acquaintance of Rahel, also a convert, Dorothea Mendelssohn Schlegel, the youngest daughter of Moses Mendelssohn.

In 1796 Rahel met Count Carl von Finckenstein, a charming, cultured, and handsome man, to whom she became passionately attached. They became engaged and for a year her head was clouded by romantic notions of what she thought he was. He was affectionate and tender but somehow could not overcome his awareness that she was penniless and a Jewess to boot. These hindrances were constantly reiterated by his adoring mother and doting sisters. Rahel offered him his freedom, but that did not satisfy him either. They remained in this indecisive state for four years during which he wrote her clumsy affectionate letters, which she at first answered passionately. Her letters to him gradually became despairing as she realized he was content with the status quo and was not prepared to go further. In 1799 this aimless relationship was finally broken off and they did not meet again until 12 years later when he called on her and introduced his wife. He felt very complacent, but she was still hurt and bitter at the pain he had caused her. He died a few months after this visit. He had destroyed all the letters she had written to him.

Fortunately Rahel was able to leave Berlin almost immediately after the breakup of this affair, when she was invited by her friend the Countess Schlabrendorf to accompany her to Paris. Here there were many distractions which gave Rahel the welcome opportunity to use her critical faculties. Those to whom she wrote were confirmed in their admiration of her sound judgment and depth of perception. Friedrich Schlegel wrote to her years later from Paris, "Here I often think of you and am reminded of what you told me of the French. You have given me the most correct, or rather the only correct description of them."

In Paris she met Wilhelm Bokelman through her friend David Veit. Bokelman was known there as "Le Beau Kelman" because of his good looks. Though he was eight years her junior and spent only two months in Paris, they formed a loving friendship. She wrote to him for a short time after he left but nothing came of it. Years later, Ludwig Varnhagen sought him out after Rahel had died and they exchanged reminiscences. Rahel left Paris by way of Amsterdam where she visited her sister who had just married a Dutchman. From Amsterdam, she returned home with her mother to resume her normal life.

Among her acquaintances at this time was Friedrich Gentz, a Romantic antisemite who corresponded with her during the rest of her life. His letters to her seemed sincere, but to others he wrote disparagingly of her. She was the Jew who was not as vile as all the rest; it was fashionable for all the well-known antisemites of the day to have their "nice Jews." The Jews of Prussia had been emancipated as a result of the Napoleonic wars. However, the Prussians who had become strongly nationalistic and were unable to vent their hatred on the French turned on the Jews. Antisemitism became fashionable again and the Jews eventually lost all their hard-won gains. Rahel naturally was ambivalent about her patriotism, having been an ardent admirer of Napoleon and everything French.

In 1801 she embarked on a brief and stormy affair with Raphael D'Urquijo, a young, handsome Spaniard with the legation in Berlin. She was now 30, a romantic, intelligent and sensitive woman. D'Urquijo wanted to marry her but her independent spirit would not submit to his possessive, domineering attitude. It was during this period, in 1803, that she first met Karl Auguste Varnhagen von Ense, who was then a penniless young student. She left a deep and lasting impression on the young man, and in his memoirs he tells of their first meeting. "There appeared a light graceful figure, small but well built, with delicate rounded limbs. Her hands and feet were strikingly small, her face, surrounded by a wealth of thick hair, showed her mental superiority; the quick yet steady glance of the dark eyes caused one to wonder whether they revealed or received more; an expression of suffering lent to her dear features a gentle charm." Varnhagen did not see Rahel again until the spring of 1807 when they met at a friend's home. He also saw her with her brother at Fichte's lectures, but being a little bashful, did not approach her. Finally, in 1808, he met her walking on "Unter den Linden" and took the opportunity to speak to her. She invited him to call, which he did without delay. He became deeply attached to her, but she was wary because of disappointments already suffered; moreover, Varnhagen himself was ambivalent as he hoped to make a name for himself in the diplomatic corps and did not wish to go through life just as "Rahel's husband." However, they corresponded extensively. When war broke out between Austria and France in 1809, Varnhagen joined the army to fight for Austria. After the defeat of Wagram he accompanied his commanding officer Colonel Bentheim to Prague, Paris, and Vienna and formed useful connections with influential men, among them Metternich.

Rahel's interest in Goethe led to yet another occupation for Varnhagen. He began to collect everything Rahel had ever written to him about Goethe and sent it to a publisher, who would not publish it without Goethe's personal opinion. Goethe was favorably impressed and wrote Rahel a letter of recommendation. The correspondence between Rahel and Varnhagen was published in 1812, establishing both firmly in the world of letters. Rahel met Goethe twice, once in 1796 briefly in the park at Karlsbad, and the second and last time in Frankfurt in 1815, when he called on her unannounced, shortly after her marriage to Varnhagen, a visit she recorded in detail.

Meanwhile, Rahel was forced to leave Berlin because of the war and make her way to Prague, where she found she possessed a genuine talent for fund-raising and organization. She comforted, consoled, advised, and gave whatever limited funds she had unstintingly to the many people who were left homeless and ill. However, the emotional and physical strain was too great; she became ill and was forced to discontinue these activities.

It was not until June of 1814 that she met Varnhagen again. Her conversion in order to marry him took place in Teplitz in September, 1814 and on the same day they were married. She was 43 years old and he 13 years younger. He continued as a diplomat, not very successfully, and his career ended abruptly in 1819 when he was pensioned off.

They returned to Berlin where, once settled, it was impossible for Rahel not to become a magnet for many intellectuals of the city. People came to talk and to exchange critical, cultural, and political ideas. Although this salon never possessed quite the excitement or the fascination of her attic room, many old friends drifted back. Among her visitors were the philosopher Hegel, the historian Ranke, and the poet Heinriche Heine, who called Rahel "the most inspired woman of the universe." She was totally absorbed in the world of ideas, aware of any new movement in the arts as well as in politics. Unasked, Beethoven once played for her for several hours, and he was not known to waste his genius on the unappreciative. Varnhagen himself finally found his niche. Although he bitterly regretted his forced retirement from the diplomatic ranks, he read voraciously, began to write and became known as an astute literary critic.

Life became outwardly very placid. Rahel was devoted to her brother's children and grandchildren, being childless herself. Her family ties and intellectual activities occupied her completely until her death in 1833 at the age of 62.

Rahel was the epitome of the true romantic, with extreme sensibility, falling in love with handsome young men many years her junior and writing letters and journals with ardent candor and exceptional style. She wanted to be a writer but knew she was not sufficiently gifted. Nevertheless, she was one of the earliest critics to realize the greatness of Goethe and was one of the people who helped establish his great reputation. She understood Goethe's works completely, and his name appeared frequently in her diary and letters as her teacher, friend, and idol. Varnhagen, having helped her create the Goethe cult, was just as successful in fabricating a Rahel Varnhagen cult after her death. He lived on until 1858, devoting the rest of his life to cherishing her memory. He published her letters and diaries, as well as his own recollections of everything she had done.

Her historical importance lies in the fact that he succeeded in gathering together all her letters from their recipients and theirs to her and forming a collection of manuscripts describing the thoughts, feelings, and interests of the important figures who were part of the Romantic period in Prussia. It was called the Varnhagen Collection and was housed in the Prussian State Library. Unfortunately it has since disappeared.

Rahel hated being Jewish and had ascribed to Judaism all the griefs and disappointments of her life. Toward the end of her life, however, she had modified this harsh judgment, telling Varnhagen, "What for so long a period of my life seemed to me the greatest shame, the harshest suffering and misfortune, namely that I was born a Jewess, I would not now renounce for any price." She had apparently come to realize that all she was, all she had contributed, all her gifts were due to her Jewish heritage. Perhaps this explains why after her death Varnhagen gave a large sum of money to the Jewish poor in her memory.

In a way Rahel Lewin Varnhagen's personal history was a reflection of the tragic history of the Jews in Germany right down to its conclusion in the twentieth century: the basically Romantic ideas of assimilation with their corresponding self-hatred, the urge to leave and forget the Jewish heritage and background, and later the realization that this was impossible because the outside world never permitted it.

Rebecca Gratz

Rebecca Gratz, a prominent member of a large and illustrious family of the antebellum period in the United States was a woman of culture, active in all kinds of philanthropic work, a devoted Jewess, and a prolific writer of letters. She was the ideal of her family and beloved and admired by all who knew her.

Rebecca was born on March 4, 1781 in Philadelphia, the daughter of Michael Gratz, originally from Langendorf, Germany, and Miriam Simon of Lancaster, Pennsylvania. It was a marriage of two of the most important business families of Pennsylvania, the Gratz's of Philadelphia and Joseph Simon, the principal merchant of Lancaster. The marriage was performed by Gershon Seixas, *hazzan* of Shearith Israel (the Spanish and Portuguese Synagogue) of New York in 1769.

Brought up in the strict faith of orthodox Judaism, Rebecca never swerved from the religion of her fathers throughout her life even though intermarriage was rife among her cousins and brothers. Rebecca was one of 12 children many of whom became people of note. Principal among them was her brother Hyman who, unmarried, left his money and estate for the founding of a college (Gratz College) for the education of Jews residing in the city of

Philadelphia. The most famous of the twelve, however, was Rebecca.

Like all women in those days, Rebecca received very little formal education. However, she was very well read and conversant with Burns, Pope, Milton, Oliver Goldsmith, Scott, and most of the English literature of the day. Moreover, she was an excellent letter writer and corresponded widely. She was accustomed from early childhood to be among the famous people of her time which included writers, politicians, and the wealthy. The Ogdens, Gouverneurs, Hoffmans, Fennos, Washington Irving, James Paulding, Sam Ewing, and Henry Clay were just a few of the famous people with whom she was on friendly terms. In addition, members of the family were painted by all the famous artists of the day including Sully and Gilbert Stuart. She was an elegant, cultured woman, good natured, showing consideration to everyone around her.

Rebecca Gratz is said to have been the model for the heroine of the novel *Ivanhoe* by Sir Walter Scott, whose attention had been drawn to her character by Washington Irving. This was believed and written about by her family; however, Rebecca never identified herself as the heroine in any of her voluminous correspondence. Neither have we found any letters of Washington Irving or Sir Walter Scott to give any credence to the story. On the other hand, there is no proof that the story is not true. Further proof via a letter of Washington Irving or Sir Walter Scott may finally decide the matter.

No doubt her personal life did resemble, in a way, the life of Rebecca of *Ivanhoe*. When Rebecca Gratz was in her early twenties she became emotionally involved with Samuel Ewing, the son of the provost of the University of Pennsylvania and one of the most promising young lawyers of the city. She attended several public affairs with him and there was no doubt that they were in love. But when the question of marriage arose, both felt that their loyalty to their respective religions made that impossible. Tearfully they agreed to part. Ewing is reported to have told Miss Redman, who became his wife in 1810, that he had deeply loved Rebecca and that only the difference in their religions prevented him from being married. Rebecca never married. When Ewing, married and the father of a family, died tragically at the age of 39 in 1825, Rebecca Gratz came quietly into the room where his body lay in its coffin, dramatically placed three white roses on his breast, put a miniature of herself next to his heart, and left as silently as she had come in. This story reveals the conflict in the heart of a beautiful and intelligent woman dedicated to her own religion at the cost of her personal happiness.

To her credit, Rebecca did not bemoan her faith or sit out her life resting on the laurels of her sacrifice to her religion. Henceforth all her energies were dedicated to philanthropic and social projects. In 1801 she was elected secretary of the Female Association for the Relief of Woman and Children in Reduced Circumstances and was among the founders of the Philadelphia Orphan Asylum in 1815. Four years later she was elected secretary of its board of managers, a position she held for 40 years. She became the guiding hand of the Female Hebrew Benevolent Society in 1819. This was the first separate charitable organization founded by Jews in Philadelphia and the oldest Jewish charity in the United States which has remained in continuous existence. In 1850, calling herself "A Daughter of Israel," she advocated in the Jewish periodical *The Occident* the foundation of a Jewish Foster Home. Her advocacy was instrumental in the establishment of such a home in 1855. She also aided in the founding of a Fuel Society in 1841 and the Ladies Hebrew Sewing Society in 1838. In all these endeavors she not only offered her labor, ideas, and enthusiasm, but contributed from her personal funds as well.

Rebecca did not just devote her energies to public philanthropies. When her sister Rachael died, she made a temporary home for the bereaved father and children. In a family tragedy, she was always present in person and through sympathetic letters, soothing and giving courage through her affection and religion.

Her most notable achievement was the founding of what is probably the first Jewish Sunday school in America. The vast majority of the Jews of the United States in general and of Philadelphia in particular were growing up in total ignorance of their faith. Rebecca Gratz conceived the idea of a Sunday school, modeled after similar Christian Sunday schools, where Jewish children would receive some instruction in the essentials of Judaism. Accordingly, together with several other Jewish women, she founded a Hebrew Sunday school in 1838 and assumed the positions of teacher, superintendent, and president.

The first school was in a room on Zane Street (now Filbert Street) near Seventh Street over the Phoenix Hose Company. It was a large room with four long windows at one end. Between the center windows was a raised platform upon which stood a table and chair. On the table was a Bible containing both the Old and New Testaments (no other English Bibles were yet available), a hand bell, *Watt's Hymns,* and a penny contribution box "for the poor of Jerusalem." Here Miss Gratz presided, a stately commanding figure, always dressed neatly in plain black with thin white collar and cuffs, and close-fitting bonnet over her dark brown curls.

The benches, painted bright yellow with an arm at each end, accomodated about 10 children each. On the board across the back of the room were beautiful medallions of mills, farmhouses, etc. The instruction was principally oral in those early days. Miss Gratz always began the school day with a prayer, "Come ye Children, harken unto me, and I will teach you the fear of the Lord." This was followed by a prayer of her own composition, which she read verse by verse, and which the whole school repeated after her. Then she read a chapter from the Bible, in a clear and distinct voice which could be heard and understood all over the room. The closing exercises were equally simple; a Hebrew hymn sung by the children, then one of Watt's simple verses whose rhythm the smallest child could easily catch as all repeated, "Send me the voice that Samuel heard."

Pyke's *Catechism* with its famous opening question, "Who formed you, child, and made you live?" and the answer, "God did my life and spirit give" was the most important text of the school. The Scripture lessons were taught from a little illustrated work published by the Christian Sunday School Union. Rebecca and her family spent many long summer days pasting pieces of paper over answers unsuitable for Jewish children. Her nieces reported that many were the fruitless efforts of those children to read through, over or under the hidden lines.

Miss Gratz was then 57, an age which most people would consider too advanced to attempt a new undertaking. Yet she lived to see the school increase a great deal from a mere handful, 50 children and seven teachers, mostly of her own family and all belonging to the Mikveh Israel Congregation. When she handed it over to her successor 26 years later, there were students from every congregation in Philadelphia among the 200 pupils. This example set by the Hebrew Sunday school of Philadelphia has been taken up, and Jewish Sunday schools have spread throughout the entire country wherever a settled Jewish community exists.

Rebecca Gratz died on August 27, 1869. Her last will and testament began with these beautiful words: "I, Rebecca Gratz, of Philadelphia, being in sound health of body and mind, advanced in the vale of years, declaim this to be my last will and testament. I commit my spirit to the God who gave it, relying on His mercy and redeeming love, and believing with a firm and perfect faith in the religion of my fathers: 'Hear O Israel, the Lord our God is one Lord.' "

Rebecca Gratz's admired qualities of loyalty to religion and family and her belief in philanthropy and good deeds might be considered old-fashioned, but she was nonetheless a modern and emancipated woman. Whether or not the story of her love for a non-Jew is the reason for her staying single is uncertain. She obviously found no one she really wished to marry and instead of accepting marriage for its own sake, she defied the convention of her time and stayed an "old maid." Rather than bemoan her fate, she enjoyed life to the full, traveling, writing, making friends among the cultured people of her day; she put meaning into her existence by founding and working for various educational, social, and philanthropic organizations to better the lives of those less fortunate than herself. That she remained a loyal Jewess and worked in and for her own community should redound to her honor.

She was the first woman in American Jewish history worthy of note. At a time when Jewish men, let alone Jewish women, were not attuned to literature and culture, Rebecca Gratz sought these out, both in her own reading and study and in her personal relationships. At a time when the cultured Jewesses of Europe left their faith and heritage, Rebecca Gratz staunchly defended it. When American Jewish men sincerely concerned about the lack of Jewish education for the vast majority of Jewish youth just threw up their hands in despair, it was Rebecca Gratz who almost singlehandedly did something about the situation.

She founded an institution that soon swept the country and still exists today. For hundreds of thousands of Jewish children, the Jewish Sunday school provided the only link they had with their Jewish heritage. She can hardly be faulted for the fact that the educational value of these Sunday schools leaves much to be desired. That fault must lie at the doorstep of the communal rabbis and educators who just took what she gave them without attempting to attain greater religious educational goals. She planted an "acorn"; they never tended the seedling which forever remained just an "acorn." Had this small acorn blossomed, as it could very well have, into a network of Jewish schools with a rich program in Judaic studies, she would have been acknowledged as truly great. However, in her time, in her sphere, in her milieu, Rebecca did more than anyone else could possibly have done for the furtherance of Jewish education. For that she unquestionably deserves to be considered among the notable women of Jewish history.

Ernestine Rose

Ernestine Louise Rose, a well-known name a century ago, is now almost completely forgotten. In her day she was considered a radical for espousing such unpopular causes as women's rights, the abolition of slavery, and free public education. Newspaper reporters jeered at her, editors disliked her, and clergymen hated her, but they were all unable to ignore her charm and eloquence as a speaker and debator.

Ernestine Louise Siismundi Potowski was born January 13, 1810 in the ghetto of Piotrkow, Poland, the daughter of a rabbi. There is no doubt that in her youth she witnessed the misery, suffering, and injustice of the Jews of the ghetto. Poland was then divided among Austria, Prussia and Russia. Piotrkow had fallen under the rule of the Russian Czar, but discrimination and mistreatment against the Jews were the same in all parts of Poland. Although in 1810 half the population of Piotrkow was Jewish, the ghetto comprised a very small part of the town, occupying a marshy area on the east bank of the river Strava.

As an only child, Ernestine was precocious, intelligent, and eager to learn the Hebrew subjects which her father taught her. After her mother's death, when she was 16, her father attempted to marry her off without her consent, but she refused. Subsequently, her father himself married a young girl about the same age as Ernestine. The situation became untenable and Ernestine left home, never to return.

She arrived in Berlin in 1827 and lived there for two years. It is not unlikely that she earned her livelihood by giving Hebrew lessons. She supplemented her earnings selling chemically treated paper which dispelled odors when burned. During her stay she learned to speak German fluently.

In June 1829, aged 19, she left Germany, traveling through Holland, Belgium, and France. While she was in Holland a petition was circulated to free a poor woman wrongly imprisoned. Ernestine willingly espoused this cause, perhaps her first cause, actively seeking names for the petition. During her stay in France, she heard about an uprising in Poland and attempted to return home. When she was stopped at Coblentz, a city on the Rhine, she went on to England where a quiet but far-reaching social revolution was taking place.

Robert Owen had taken over a poverty-stricken factory community in New Lanark in 1800 which he had transformed into a profit-making model city. Homes were built for the workers, a school was set up for their children, and working conditions were improved. The town became a magnet for reformers, educators, and even royalty who wished to see Owen's theories put into practice. Owen tried to start a commune in Louisiana but the experiment failed miserably and he returned to England in 1829. Ernestine had become interested in Owenism and had attended many meetings concerned with it. She began to speak up at these meetings, at first haltingly because of her accent and poor vocabulary, later more frequently and with greater fluency. At these gatherings she met William Ella Rose, a jeweler and silversmith three years younger than she, an ardent Owenite like herself, whom she married some time between 1832 and 1836. In 1836 they sailed to the United States.

Almost immediately, Ernestine was plunged into what was to become her life's work. In 1836 Judge Thomas Hertell introduced a bill in the New York State Legislature to protect the rights and property of married women. Ernestine tried to obtain signatures for a petition endorsing this bill, to be sent to the State Legislature. In five months, after countless house calls, insults, and doors slammed in her face, she had five signatures. The next year she tried again. For four years Ernestine Rose trudged through middle-class neighborhoods knocking on doors, informing women of their disadvantaged position. Gradually the number of signatures increased. She joined forces with Paulina Wright Davis and Elizabeth Cady Stanton. These three women, along with Frances Wright, became the founders of the Women's Rights Movement in America.

Meanwhile the Roses had moved in 1837 to 484 Grand Street, at that time a pleasant residential neighborhood. William Rose established his business at the same address listing himself as a silversmith. A year later he moved his business to 9 Frankfort Street near Tammany Hall, where he repaired jewelry, watches, and ornaments, as well as manufacturing and selling silver. Ernestine supplemented the family income by selling eau de cologne. This, together with the fact that she knew how to fabricate impregnated paper that dispelled odors, would lead us to suspect that contrary to what she claimed, Ernestine came from a family of perfumers.

Ernestine now began to speak before committees of the New York State Legislature and to any group who would vouchsafe her a hearing. Powerful support for women's property rights came from an unexpected quarter. Anxious to keep their estates intact for their children and grandchildren, the wealthy Dutch of New York State began to back the bill. However, it was not until 1848 that the Bill for the More Effectual Protection of the Property Rights of

Women became law. Although now somewhat more secure financially, women still did not have equal rights to the custody of their own children. Previously a woman had virtually no guardianship rights over her children. The husband, or in some cases the grandfather was the guardian and could take the children away from their mother. Under the new law, women gained some but not complete, custodial rights.

In the summer of 1837, with an established reputation as an accomplished speaker, Ernestine Rose participated in a debate entitled, "To What Extent May a Community of Property be Applied to the Happiness of Mankind." Ernestine was on for the entire course, while new adversaries debated her each week. The organization sponsoring this debate was a group of reformers and freethinkers known as the Society for Moral Philanthropists. They formed the circle in which Ernestine moved.

In 1843 she attended a convention sponsoring an Owenite commune in Skaneateles, New York. She became a roving ambassador for the community, trying to raise funds and interest people, but the experiment was doomed from the start. The commune was completely ostracized by the surrounding villages, and its members bickered constantly among themselves about theory, putting very little effort into farming. However, the experiment which lasted three years ended in good shape financially because the land had doubled in value and thus more than covered all the liabilities.

Traveling throughout the country, Ernestine never failed to speak out for social reform and women's rights. In 1846 she went to Michigan on a lecture tour, speaking twice in Ann Arbor at the Hall of the House of Representatives. An excellent female speaker, a rarity in those days, always attracted an audience whether it agreed with the subject or not. Lectures in the United States were then and still are a popular form of entertainment, and Ernestine who recognized this fact never refused an invitation to speak, even to the smallest group, because a convert to her point of view might be found anywhere and she realized that women's rights and social reforms would not be achieved easily. While in Kentucky she contracted ague, a form of malaria common all over Europe and America, which lasted several months, and the following year went to Charleston, South Carolina, to recuperate. Appalled by the sight of slavery, she placed an advertisement in the local newspaper inviting the public to a lecture, the subject of which was the desirability of abolition. Only the fact that she was a woman prevented her from being lynched. She was forced to leave Charleston rather precipitously.

In 1850 Ernestine Rose was one of the principal speakers at the first Women's Rights Convention in Worcester, Massachusetts, organized by Lucretia Mott, Martha C. Wright, and Elizabeth Cady Stanton. It was attended by women interested in their rights and by abolitionists with whom, at this time, they appeared to have much in common. Ernestine Rose spoke several times extemporaneously, introducing one of the resolutions, but there is no record of any of her speeches except in the articles of the reporters present. The convention was lampooned in the press and fiercely derided from the pulpit.

Every year since their arrival in the United States, William and Ernestine Rose had attended the Tom Paine Birthday dinner and dance, and in 1850 Ernestine was invited to be the keynote speaker. Approximately 800 people attended this affair, at the cost of a dollar per person. This dinner was sponsored by freethinkers and Ernestine's speech was on their philosophy which held that opinions on religion may be formed independently of the established tradition. Both the *New York Herald* and the *Cincinnati Non-pareil* violently disagreed with her speech, but called her an excellent speaker, much more accomplished than most men.

Ernestine spent the year 1851 traveling throughout New York State, speaking in church halls and at any gathering that would give her a hearing. After her speeches many clergymen would get up to refute what she had said. The clergymen were even against free puplic education, claiming that the schools were a haven for radicals and freethinkers. Unperturbed, Ernestine would retort that the truth sounds better when surrounded by severe criticism. Once, in response to a newspaper attack by a Unitarian clergyman over her view on Women's Rights, she wrote back wondering about the low opinions the clergyman held of his female parishioners, his mother, his wife, and his daughters. Her speaking tour culminated at the second Women's Rights Convention held at Worcester, Massachusetts, in October. Her speech, lasting over an hour, was given to an appreciative, spellbound audience in a packed hall, and Paulina Wright Davis recalled many years later that hers was the best lecture of the convention. L.E. Barnard described her in these words: "She had a rich musical voice with just enough foreign accent and idiom to add to the charm of her oratory. As a speaker she was pointed, logical and impassioned. She not only dealt in abstract principles clearly, but in their application touched with the deepest emotions of the human soul."

In succeeding years, the Women's Rights Conventions were disrupted often by clergymen who were consistently against women's rights. They earnestly believed that the inferiority of women was ordained by the Bible, and they quoted copiously from its pages. Many of the women, though not all, were radicals and freethinkers, something that caused the clergymen great concern. In Bangor, Maine, a heated fight broke out between two clergymen, one of whom was determined not to allow Ernestine Rose to speak in the town. He accused her of being an atheist and a Jewess, and labeling her as lower than a prostitute, said the worst strumpet was more respectable than she. The vicious attack backfired; her ability to speak without notes and her quiet mode of dress won over not only her audience but all the reporters present. However, even within the ranks of the women's rights movement, Ernestine Rose was considered a radical. Her outspoken opinions as a freethinker did not endear her to the moderates who felt she impeded women's rights more than she helped the cause. But her position as their most important speaker ensured that she was not dropped from the roster of members.

In May of 1855 William and Ernestine Rose left for a well-deserved vacation in Europe. They visited Robert Owen at his home outside London and made all the well-known tourist stops including Madame Tussard's Waxworks. In Paris, they met Madame Jenny P. d'Hericourt, a physician and reformer who later wrote a short biography of Ernestine. It is known that Ernestine visited her relatives in Italy and Germany, but she probably did not go to Poland. The Roses returned six months later, toward the end of the year, just in time to attend a convention held in New York. Ernestine gave an account of her trip and described the status of women in Europe, also pointing out that in some countries not all men had voting rights.

It was about this time that the newspapers began equating women's rights with free love, no doubt because the plight of the prostitute was openly discussed at these conventions. At one convention held in Rutland, Vermont, in 1858, Mrs. Julia Branch proposed a resolution attributing to marriage all the disadvantages suffered by women. Ernestine followed, refuting the argument, eloquent in her support of marriage based on love, equality, and mutual respect. The newspapers attributed the statements about free love to Ernestine and she had a difficult time rebutting the accusations.

The movement was just beginning to achieve respectability; several wealthy people donated money, and many distinguished people were attracted to the cause, the most prominent among them, the Reverend Henry Ward Beecher. Finally, in 1860 the New York State Legislature passed an "Act concerning the Rights and Liabilities of Husband and Wife," granting married women full property rights and equal guardianship of the children, but no voting rights.

Immediately following this triumph the women turned their attention to the divorce laws. There was violent opposition to the subject among them. Ernestine Rose backed Elizabeth Cady Stanton and Susan B. Anthony in favor of easing the law. However, all their projects were held in abeyance because abolition occupied the center of attention for the next four years. During the Civil War, while the women were occupied with other matters, the New York State Legislature sneaked through a slight change in the law which in effect negated women's guardianship rights. These were not achieved again until many years later.

During this period Ernestine Rose, who had no contact with Jews or the Jewish community, rose in their defense when her radical friend, Horace Seaver, editor of the *Boston Investigator*, wrote an editorial that the Jews "were about the worst people of whom we have any account. . . ," that Judaism was "bigoted, narrow, exclusive and totally unfit for a progressive people like the Americans among whom we hope it may not spread. . ." Since she was a frequent contributor to the newspaper, her reply was published, but it was divided into two installments with antisemitic rebuttals at the end of each, thus lessening its impact. The controversy dragged on for 10 weeks with the Jewish weeklies commenting from the sidelines. Until this episode many people had not even realized that she was Jewish. Judaism simply had not played a part in her life.

After the Civil War, the women's rights movement suffered its greatest setback; the abolitionists, having achieved their own ends, abandoned them. The male Negro had been given the vote, women had not. The women in the movement were extremely bitter over their betrayal. All the prominent men who in the past had supported their cause now withdrew from the movement. Frederick Douglass, Wendell Philips, Horace Greeley, and Henry Ward Beecher. The movement was split over whether to push for women's suffrage or just to improve their general living conditions. The breach took some 20 years to heal.

Ernestine Rose, whose health had been deteriorating, played no part in the dissension within the movement. Her speaking was restricted because of neuralgia and arthritis. In 1869, when she was 60 years old, she and her husband left for England, returning once only to sell their home and its contents. Since citizenship for women held no benefits, Ernestine had not bothered to apply for it until a few months before her departure, although her husband had become a citizen a few years after their arrival in the United States. After they left, the new state of Wyoming granted women equal rights with men, including the right to vote, but it was another 50 years before all women were allowed to vote throughout the United States.

The Roses traveled all over Europe and then settled in Bath, England, for a short time. Their final destination, however, was London. Ernestine continued to speak occasionally, giving a memorial lecture for Robert Owen attended by an estimated 1,000 people. A reporter for one of the newspapers characterized her as the foremost lady orator of the day. In 1882, William Rose died and was buried in Highgate, a nonsectarian cemetary. Ernestine died in Brighton 10 years later where she was spending the summer and was buried next to her husband.

Her will was probated on December 13, 1892. In it she had left the bulk of her estate to three married nieces whose family name had been Morganstern. The will is something of a surprise, when one realizes there is absolutely no other mention of members of her family; she claimed she had been an only child. Three possibilities come to mind; the first and highly unlikely supposition is that they were the children of a half-sister. However, having chosen to leave her family, it does not seem likely that she would have maintained contact. If the nieces were from her side of the family, we must deduce that she was not an only child and that the few details she made known of her early life are untrue. If they were the daughters of William Rose's sister, it is highly likely that he was, contrary to current opinion, also of Jewish descent.

Ernestine Rose was the outstanding speaker and debater of the Women's Rights Movement and as one of its founders deserves greater recognition that has been accorded her. The reason for her almost complete eclipse is that she was a private, secretive individual, one who felt as insecure with the written word as she was proficient with the spoken word. Even when Susan B. Anthony started assembling material for a history of the Women's Rights movement in the United States and wrote to Ernestine in 1876 requesting biographical information, Ernestine sent only a few details of the places where she had spoken. Although Ernestine was a radical and a freethinker, considered an extremist even among those women actively fighting for their rights, she was their best, most indefatigable, and most lucid defender. They were in no position at any time to be able to dispense with her services. Many people disagreed with her point of view and jeered at her speeches, but she was always able to hold the attention of large audiences and gain their respect for her abilities.

She never denied her Jewish background; it just had no place in her life. However, unable to stomach the vicious lying attacks on Jews, even from a close friend, she rose in their defense although it meant breaking off the friendship. Ernestine Rose's aim in life was, in her own words, "to do my duty in defense of justice." This she did, single-mindedly, all her life.

The Maid of Ludomir

Today it is commonly taken for granted that one of the last strongholds of male chauvinism is among the Hassidim, the extreme right ultra-religious mystical sect of Orthodox Judaism. This is a man's religion, with the rebbe or tsaddik at the head, conducting *tish* (public meals) for his male adherents and distributing *shirayim* (gleanings of his meal). He receives petitions from his followers, dispenses advice, and is considered so holy as to be in almost constant communion with the Almighty.

Hassidism was founded in the Russian Ukraine in the early eighteenth century by a man of humble origins and with relatively little formal education. Israel Baal Shem Tov (or, by abbreviation, Besht) taught that all Jews were equal before God, the unlearned as well as the scholars, and that prayers and humility were more acceptable in Heaven than intellectual achievements. His most important teaching was that the true way of serving God is through cheerfulness, happiness and song. After the Besht's death, the movement was continued by his disciples, each one leading his own group. They became known as rebbes (a title for the leader) or tsaddikim (used as a descriptive term for a holy man). Hassidism relies heavily on mysticism and the rebbe or tsaddik was considered to be not only a man of righteous precepts but a worker of miracles and unrivaled spiritual authority. One would imagine that this is certainly no place for a woman, who could never aspire to become a rebbe or tsaddik. The undisputed facts, however, prove the exact opposite. Nothing in the theory of Hassidism can prevent a woman from rising to the rank of tsaddik. In fact, several women became rebbes and leaders in their own right. They wore *tzitzit* (ritual fringes), put on *tiffilin,* fasted on Mondays and Thursdays, conducted *tish,* and were reputed to be able to accomplish great deeds.

The most famous of all the Hassidic women rebbes was unquestionably Hannah Rachel (c. 1815-92), immortalized in Hassidic legends under the name of "The Maid of Ludomir." Her biography reads like a tale of unbelievable mysticism, rivaling the biographies of any of the most important rebbes. She was born in Ludomir, Poland, the daughter of Monesh Werbemacher, a man of means and education. An only child, she received the attention usually reserved for an eldest son, including much more education that was usually given girls at this time. She especially excelled in the study of Midrash, an ethical and devotional explanation of Biblical texts, Aggada, stories, moral fables, history from the Talmud, and the books of Musar, which concerned moral disciplines.

It was reported that due to his position and wealth, her father was approached by many matchmakers who proposed marvelous matches for her from other towns. However, her father refused all their offers and chose a young man in his own town whom Hannah Rachel had known and loved from her earliest childhood. It is claimed that she longed to be alone with her fiancé, to tell him of her feelings, but that this was an impossibility, according to the customs of the time; the meeting of engaged couples before marriage was prohibited.

Hannah Rachel's mother died at about this time. The girl, who probably had confided in her mother, now became withdrawn and solitary and fell prey to moods of melancholy. She sat all day long in her room and went out only to visit the grave of her mother, where she would cry her heart out. Once, legend says, after a particularly long and tiring talk at the graveside, she fell asleep. When she awoke it was pitch dark and there was no one to be seen. The eerie shapes and shadows of the kingdom of death terrified her. She began to run home and in her semi-conscious state stumbled over one of the headstones and fell into a half-filled grave. Terrified, she screamed and fainted. The old sexton heard her cry, found her, and carried her to her father's house. She went into severe shock, hovering for a long time on the brink of death. For many days she did not speak at all. The physicians had given up all hope for her recovery when one day she asked for her father and announced to him that she had just been in Heaven at a sitting of the highest court where she had received a new and sublime soul. Within a few days, she seemed completely recovered. Thereafter, she put on tzitzit, wrapped herself in a talit, and put on tiffilin, activities reserved just for men. She also spent the entire day studying Torah and praying. Quite understandably her betrothal was annulled.

When her father died soon after, Hannah Rachel recited the traditional kaddish for him, another activity usually reserved only for male relatives. With the considerable fortune that he left her, she built a new *beth ha-medrash* (prayer and study house) with an adjoining apartment for her living quarters. The entire week she used to sit in her quarters praying and studying the Torah. Every Sabbath at *shalosh seudot* (the third meal usually near the conclusion of the sabbath), the door of the apartment would be opened. The unseen "Maid of Ludomir" would deliver erudite and Hassidic discourse for the Hassidim who would gather at her *tish*.

Soon her fame spread far and wide. Thousands of men

and women made pilgrimages to her *beth ha-medrash* as
Christians did to a saint; even learned men, rabbis, and
other tsaddikim came to hear her. Gradually a special
group of Hassidim was formed which became known as the
"Hassidim of the Maid of Ludomir." They used to pray in
her *beth ha-medrash* and treat her as all other Hassidim
treated their tsaddik. She became known as a miracle
worker who, among other miracles, could cure the sick. In-
deed, she gave curative herbs to the sick who came to her.

The other tsaddikim were astounded by their new colleague and after a while became somewhat uneasy. Some
wondered whether there was not an "evil spirit" in this
strange virgin. Others were no doubt jealous of her success.
Most were probably sincerely apprehensive that she might
become a model for other Jewish women in remaining unmarried, which due to the sparsity of Jews in the world
could become a dangerous threat to Jewish survival. They
tried to convince her to marry, but with little success.

At the age of 40 she succumbed to the persuasive arguments of a celebrated tsaddik, Rabbi Mordecai of Czernobiel, and agreed to marry a Talmudic scholar recommended by him. Why she gave in and decided to marry at
her advanced (for that period) age can only be conjectured.
It could have been the pressure of constant urgings by the
other tsaddikim or boredom with her life or some clever
words of Rabbi Mordecai who might have played on her
credulity in believing she might conceive and bring forth a
"savior of Israel." Whatever the reason, soon after her marriage her influence waned. The marriage was short-lived
and terminated by divorce and Hannah Rachel emigrated
to Palestine.

There, it was reported, she met a famous Cabbalist.
Together they resolved by various Cabbalistic and Hassidic
machinations to end the Jewish exile and hasten the coming
of the Messiah. After long, hard, and elaborate preparation

a time and place was set for the final enactment of their work. The Maid of Ludomir arrived punctually at the appointed place, a cave outside Jerusalem. The third man, required by the Jewish law which prohibits a man and woman to be alone in a secluded place or room, also arrived on time. But the aged Cabbalist did not arrive. It was reported that he had set out on time for the meeting. A short way from his house he met a very old Jew with a long white beard who asked the Cabbalist for something to eat. Happy to perform the *Mitzvah* of hospitality to a stranger, he invited him to his home. They began to talk and, being old, the Cabbalist completely forgot about his appointment. The old man was Elijah, the prophet, in disguise. The apocalyptic plot was foiled. The Messianic era could not be hastened!

To us it may seem that the Maid of Ludomir was a slightly eccentric nonconformist. However, she was part of the mainstream of mysticism, the basis of Hassidism, no different from the sainted Besht and other famous rebbes. Erudite, a mystic who possessed considerable charisma, she was able to overcome the strict and confining limitation which the ghetto imposed on women to become a famous Hassidic leader. Had she been able to resolve the problem of marriage or spinsterhood, she might have become one of the greatest of the rebbes. As it is, she can lay claim to being a most noteworthy Hassidic leader, one of the most original, and the first to settle in the Holy Land. She not only dreamt of hastening the end of the Jewish exile, but actually attempted to accomplish it.

Rachel

Asked to name a great tragic actress, most people would think quickly of Sarah Bernhardt, a familiar name in America even today. While Sarah Bernhardt enjoys a justifiable fame, however, the first truly great tragedienne in whose footsteps Bernhardt followed remains in obscurity.

We tend to picture tragic actresses as tall majestic figures, but the greatest tragic actress of all time, Rachel, was a slight, slim, tiny figure who was able to dominate a stage with her personality and talent and who singlehandedly revitalized the classical French repertoire which had been dormant for many years for want of talent.

Born Elisa Félix in 1821 in the village of Mumpf, Switzerland, Rachel was the daughter of a Jewish peddlar, Jacob Félix, and his wife Esther Haya and was one of six surviving children. For 10 years the family wandered through Germany and Switzerland with Jacob eking out a meager existence hawking cheap goods wherever he could.

In 1831 the family finally settled down, first in Lyons and later in Paris. To augment the Félix budget, Elisa and her older sister Sarah sang in the streets. In 1832, while out for a stroll, Etienne Choron, a well-known music teacher, heard them and took them under his wing. He enrolled them in his music school where they received musical training as well as an elementary education.

Elisa had little aptitude as a singer but was very gifted as an actress and so was passed on by M. Choron in 1834 to M. Saint-Aulaire who ran an academy of dramatic art. Blessed with a prodigious memory, she was able to learn all the roles of the classic repertory with ease. On her fifteenth birthday she was presented by M. Saint-Aulaire to M. Jouslin de la Salle, then director of the Comédie Française. Having passed an audition, she was engaged to play child roles at an annual salary of 800 francs ($200), and was also permitted to attend classes at the Conservatoire. However, she was given only the most trifling parts, which left her deeply unhappy.

After four months Elisa was introduced, again through M. Saint-Aulaire, to the manager of the Gymnase Théâtre who gave her her first real chance. Her salary, large for a beginner, rose from 4,000 to 6,000 francs within two years. It was while Elisa played at the Gymnase that she was induced to drop the commonplace name of Elisa in favor of the stage name Rachel. This strikingly Jewish euphonious, and easily remembered name was borrowed from Halévy's popular opera *La Juive*. Unfortunately, there were no plays in the Gymnase's repertory that suited Rachel's classic style which forced her to return to the Comédie Francaise for 4,000 francs a year. She made her debut on June 12, 1838 in the role of Camille in Corneille's tragedy *Les Horaces*. Additional appearances were made during July and August for a total of 18 performances, but as the real theatre patrons and critics were all away for summer vacation Rachel made no impression.

In September the critics returned to award her outstanding reviews. Most important, the influential critic of the *Journal des Débats* Jules Janin, wrote that Rachel was the most astonishing little girl (she was only 17 years old and less than five feet tall) that the stage had to offer. People flocked to see her. Her salary was raised to 30,000 francs a year. In five months she appeared in six plays of the classic repertory: Corneille's *Les Horaces* and *Cinna*; Racine's *Andromaque, Iphigénie,* and *Mithridate;* and Voltaire's *Tancrède.* She now attempted the most demanding role of Roxane in Racine's *Bajazet*—and flopped. However, with her consummate artistry, in spite of advice to the contrary, she repeated the role shortly after and scored an amazing triumph. She was now acclaimed an acting genius.

There were constant additions to her repertory: *Esther, Nicomède, Polyeucte, Le Cid, Phèdre, Bérénice,* and *Athalie.* After completely mastering all the classic roles, she turned to the newer plays such as Pierre Lebrun's *Marie Stuart,* Latour-Saint-Ybors' *Virginie,* and Scribe and Legouvé's *Adrienne Lecouvreur.*

Among the warmest of Rachel's admirers were her own co-religionists. They patronized her performances and were always present in large numbers on any night she performed. Often she acted in dramas just for them, for example, the play *Esther* which she used to do annually when the festival of Purim came around.

She made frequent tours of France and then of Europe, including London, Brussels, Amsterdam, The Hague, Vienna, Berlin, Rome, Warsaw, and St. Petersburg. Her excellence as an actress was proclaimed by critics the world over. Matthew Arnold considered her the greatest actress ever to have lived. The *London Times* best summed up her acting by writing that a rarer combination of intelligence and power had seldom been seen. Continuing, the *Times* wrote that considering that in her youth she was almost uneducated and that her conception of tragic character was originally owing to her own genius, she may be considered a unique psychological phenomenon.

Rachel had become an extremely wealthy woman. However, her private life was scandalous. During her short lifetime she had numerous affairs; she was the mistress at times of Dr. Véron, Alfred de Musset, Prince de Joinville, Prince Jerome, Prince Napoleon (son of Prince Jerome), Ponsard, Prosper Merimée, Emile de Giradin, Duc de Gramot, Louis Napoleon, Henry Mure, a colonel in the British Army, and many many more. She had two sons, Alexandre by Count Walewski, son of Napoleon and a Polish countess, and Gabriel Victor by Arthur Bertrand, son of one of Napoleon's generals. She brought up both sons as Christians even though her father wished otherwise. She never married, having said that she was quite willing to have lodgers but not proprietors. One must remember that in France in that day a husband had complete mastery over his wife and her fortune, and was able, if he wanted, to cut her off from her own money any time he wished.

However, it would be wrong to think that Rachel was only interested in amorous pursuits. Always seeking fresh effects and learning parts for new plays, she would rehearse the slightest as well as the most important details with an unwearying resolve not to stop until she was completely satisfied, often spending three hours perfecting one line. Even sobs were studied as closely and as patiently as though the very success of the part depended on their being as natural as the real thing.

In 1855 Rachel was to embark on an ill-fated adventure in America. Prompted partly by pride and partly by money, she left France in July never again to return as an actress. She had scored successes all over Europe including Russia. America alone was left to be conquered. In addition, she hoped to make a fortune there as did the singer Jenny Lind, but it was not to be. Not only was her appearance a flop, but she lost her health by catching a severe cold which aggravated an already existent tubercular condition. She died three years later.

Why did Rachel, one of the greatest tragediennes the world had ever produced, fail in America? Perhaps because

classical tragedy does not suit the American temperament
in the least. It is too serious, too weighty and above all too
frigid. All day Americans are occupied in business and
other occupations and when they go to the theatre they
want shows that are gay and amusing such as burlesque,
farces, and musicals so that they can gain release from and
forget the day's work. In addition, Americans are notori-
ously ill-equipped to understand foreign languages. Hardly
two percent of the population understood French and following the plays with the special translations that were
handed out, was disconcerting for the viewer as well as for
the performing artists.

Quite naturally the Jews in America took a lively interest in the actress's presence and they were most gratified to
read in the *New York Tribune* that she attended synagogue
on Yom Kippur and fasted and prayed with the rest. On
another occasion a delegation of religious Jews begged
Rachel not to produce *Adrienne Lecouvreur* on the Sabbath
as they desired very much to see the performance.

In truth Rachel rarely associated with any communal
activities of Jews. She was not at all religious, going to
synagogue only on Yom Kippur. However, she was proud
of being a Jewess and was flattered by the interest which
Jewish people took in her. It is also reported that while she
was in London in 1841 she interested herself in the movement for the repeal of Jewish Parliamentary disbarment
and influenced a noted and prominent nobleman at a
soirèe given by Queen Adelaide to support the necessary
measures. Her career was not marked by any antisemitic
discrimination. The one antisemitic outburst occurred when
Rachel had foisted four members of her own family on the
payroll of the Theatre Français. That, together with the
addition of her cousin Judith and the appointment of
Offenbach as the new orchestra conductor, prompted her
enemies to remark, "The Comédie Française is not a
theatre, it is a synagogue."

She returned to France in 1856 but due to her serious illness left soon after for Egypt whose climate was supposed to be beneficial for people with tuberculosis. However, she chose to die more quickly of consumption in France among her friends than live somewhat longer in a land where she was alone except for a doctor, cook, and maid. Accordingly, she returned to France and died there January 3, 1858.

Throughout her life many people tried to convert her to Christianity. She always listened to them but never acceded to their requests. As a result of all this attention, however, she constantly had to deny the rumors of her conversion. Once, one of her friends had the Archbishop of Paris in attendance during a performance of *Polyeucte* with its famous conversion scene just in case Rachel might follow Pauline's example. Sensing the reason for his attendance Rachel asked to be excused from reciting this speech. One must remember that during this period many famous Jews did convert: Heine the poet, the composers Mendelsohn and Offenbach, the English Prime minister Benjamin Disraeli, and the children of Adolf Crémieux, the famous French Jewish community leader and jurist who happened also to be a family friend and teacher of Rachel before she embarked on her scandalous behavior. Rachel, however, remained a Jewess to the end.

On January 2, 1858 just before the end, Sarah her sister summoned 10 Jews from Nice. The moment she was about to die they entered the bedroom chanting in Hebrew a prayer to the Almighty to have pity on the poor dying woman. Rachel awoke at the words "Hear O Israel, the Lord our God, the Lord is One." Her lips parted and in a trembling voice she repeated the solemn formula, thus affirming at her death her adherence to the faith.

At her funeral on January 11, Chief Rabbi Isidore of Paris, with whom she had occasionally discussed religion and to whose synagogue she had made donations for the purchase of silver ornaments for the Torah, delivered the funeral oration. The Jewish newspapers of the day strongly disapproved of Rachel's mode of life and one bitter comment was "All that we can say of Mlle. Rachel is that to her other immoralities she has not added that of apostasy." She left $1,274,371 francs (about $250,000), a considerable sum for those days, 5,000 francs of it for various Jewish charities.

While her private life has been severely criticized it should be remembered that her frequent change of lovers fed her vanity and supplied the variety and excitement demanded by her restless nature. In excitement and change, she like many actresses and Parisians in the world of arts and letters sought a way to escape from the prevalent malaise of the age, boredom. Also, one must not forget that publicity and remaining in the public eye were very important parts of being a famous actress. Of paramount importance was the fact that she was able to transform herself, by her genius, from an uneducated street urchin into the greatest tragic actress of her day and perhaps of any day.

Hannah G. Solomon

Hannah G. Solomon was born in Chicago in 1858, the daughter of Michael and Sara Greenebaum. Michael Greenebaum came from a small town in Germany in July of 1845. Trained as a tinsmith in Germany, he could find no work there and so decided to emigrate to America. Originally his plan was to stay for four or five years, make money, and then return home. Arriving in New York he found the climate unsuitable for his health and went to Chicago in 1847, one of the first four or five Jews to settle there. He became a salesman in a hardware store and fared so well that instead of returning to Germany he convinced his family to join him. Within a few years many members of the Greenebaum family including his brothers and parents had arrived in Chicago. He married Sarah Spiegel in 1850, a relation who also came from a small town in Germany and who was now living in New York City.

Greenebaum soon became a wealthy and prosperous hardware merchant. He and Sarah had 10 children, six daughters and four sons of whom Hannah was the fourth child. Hannah's childhood was idyllic; a large house, servants, and an abundance of food and fashionable clothes, a large friendly family atmosphere within an even larger family circle of uncles, aunts, grandparents, and cousins nearby. In her early years, Hannah attended the Zion

Temple (a reform synagogue) School instead of public
school. The curriculum included instruction in the German
language and some Hebrew. While some of her older sisters and brothers were sent abroad to German-Jewish
boarding schools in Frankfurt for more intensive education,
she attended Skinner Grammar School and then went for
two years to West Division High School. Because of her
musical abilities, however, she was given private piano lessons under the guidance of Mr. Carl Wolfsohn, one of the
finest music teachers in America, and special French lessons. Her interest in music appreciation remained with her
for the rest of her life and her knowledge of German and
French stood her in good stead in her future organizational
work. She also read widely and frequently attended the
theatre.

Her father, a committed Jew, was a strong advocate of
reform Judaism. He suggested Sunday services so that men
who were occupied with business on Saturday could have
the benefits of the rabbi's sermon. Her uncle Henry was
one of Chicago's leading civic personalities. A leader of
many organizations, he gave his money, time, and effort
for numerous charitable and civic causes. Hannah herself
thus had some background for her later organizational involvement.

In 1877, when she was only 18 years old, Hannah was
invited to join the Chicago Women's Club, the first Jewess
to be accorded this honor. Why the invitation was extended
to her can only be a subject for conjecture; perhaps it was
because she was respectable, dressed properly, came from a
prosperous Americanized home and was fairly well educated by the standards of the time. It was this seemingly in-
nocuous affiliation that changed Hannah Solomon from a
relatively unknown matron to a world-wide respected figure.

On May 14, 1879, when she was 21, Hannah married

Henry Solomon, a businessman engaged in the clothing industry. They bought a large house into which they moved together with his mother, a sister, and a bachelor brother. Hannah writes quite good naturedly that she did not mind, as this was not an unusual occurence. She had three children, two sons, one of whom was to die in 1899 at the age of 19, and a daughter. While the children were growing up she divorced herself from all outside activities. She read a lot, however, kept an extensive diary, and continued her interest in music. She was devoted to her numerous brothers and sisters, cousins, and in-laws and there were countless family parties and get-togethers. She was a noted cook and her sweet-sour fish and goose were especially prized. Her life seemed destined to be happy and entirely uneventful.

The United States Congress decided that in 1893 Chicago was to be the site for a world's fair to commemorate the 400th anniversary of the discovery of America. It became the responsibility of the Chicago Women's Club to organize and establish women's participation in this fair, and it was only natural that Hannah Solomon be delegated to represent the Jewish women and authorized to call Jewish women together by whatever means and under whatever division she thought best. However, it seemed many women objected to a purely Jewish women's section among themselves so instead of being part of the women's division, the Jewish women were placed with the Parliament of Religions. Mrs. Solomon explained that in her opinion when one used the term "Jewish" it must have a purely religious connotation, and so she felt it more fitting to be with the Parliament of Religions. A Jewish women's board was formed in 1891 with Mrs. Solomon as its chairlady.

The task of getting in touch with Jewish women throughout the country was not easy. There were no telephones, radios, televisons, or printed membership lists of women's organizations. Hannah Solomon had to devise a method of reaching the outstanding Jewish women of America. She obtained a list of the leading rabbis of the large cities and communities of the country and then wrote them personal letters requesting the names of the women in their congregations whom they felt would have the most to offer such a Parliament in the way of ability, interest and leadership. She received 90 names from the rabbis and wrote each of them a personal handwritten letter. It took a year of incessant letter writing before Hannah Solomon was satisfied that a respectable group of women would turn out. At this point, Mrs. Solomon decided not to let slip by this golden opportunity to use the occasion to establish a permanent organization, the first national Jewish women's organization in the United States and the world.

Mrs. Solomon requested two places for Jewish women on the general Parliament program. The Jewish women's board had selected as speakers Henrietta Szold, then secretary of the Jewish Publication Society and later to become one of the greatest Jewish women of the twentieth century, and Josephine Lazarus, sister of the poetess Emma Lazarus whose sonnet is on the base of the Statue of Liberty and who was, herself, and excellent writer and profound thinker. However, Mrs. Solomon was almost ensnared when the Jewish men of Chicago, who had assembled to make plans for a men's congress, invited her to merge the Jewish women's group with theirs. She went along with them, with the proviso that they accord her and her group some active participation in the program. This the men refused to do and Mrs. Solomon withdrew.

The Jewish Women's Congress was a success. Twenty-nine cities were represented by 93 women. At the closing session Julia Richman of New York brought in a resolution that the delegates pledge themselves "to the support of any permanent organization which shall be the outgrowth of this Congress." Next came the problem of a name. The title "National Council of Jewish Women" was suggested and immediately adopted. A suitable program "to make a vital contribution to the religious, educational and philanthropic work of Jewry" was adopted and Hannah Solomon was immediately elected president, a post she held for 13 years. By the next convention (they assembled triennially) in New York, there were 53 sections and 3,000 members. They adopted the motto "Faith and Humanity" and a badge or pin which is still worn. Today the National Council of Jewish Women has about 60,000 members from all over the country, dedicated to "furthering human welfare in the Jewish and general communities, locally, nationally and internationally." At its latest convention its four principal resolutions were: justice for children, protection of constitutional rights of the individual, an NCJW center for research in education of the disadvantaged in Israel, and a strengthening of quality of Jewish life.

In 1894 the Council of Jewish Women became an affiliate of the National Council of Women which was organized in 1888 by Elizabeth Cady Stanton. The National Council of Women was also a member of the International Council which had, in 1893, 35 foreign countries as chapters. Hannah Solomon thus became acquainted and friendly with all the greatest women's rights advocates of the time including Susan B. Anthony and Carrie Chapman Catt.

On one of her European trips Mrs. Solomon aided the establishment of an English Jewish women's group which developed into the Union of Jewish Women of England. This marked the beginning of organization of Jewish women abroad.

In 1904 she was elected as a delegate of the National Council of Women to a meeting of the International Council of Women in Berlin. Because of her fluency in the three official languages used, English, German, and French, she became chairman of the nomination committee and the un-official translator for Susan B. Anthony, the most celeb-rated of the women delegates. Hannah Solomon's linguistic abilities generated a considerable amount of publicity and enhanced her work as delegate to many European gather-ings.

During her visit to Rome that same year she and her husband took a tour of Europe. She has written of her ex-citement when they received tickets to attend an audience with Pope Pius X. After purchasing certain clothing to comply with Vatican regulations they were granted, to-gether with 30 others, an "audience." She tells that at a sign all knelt, and as he passed each one kissed his large emerald ring, naively rationalizing her actions with the ex-planation that for some it was a religious rite; for others a mark of respect or merely a prescribed ceremony.

Hannah Solomon was active in many other charitable endeavors. In addition to the Chicago Women's Club and her most important and lasting achievement, the Council of Jewish Women, she was among the leaders of the Bureau of the Associated Charities of Chicago which later became the Bureau of Personal Services; president of the Illinois Industrial School for Girls, which later became the Park Ridge School for Girls; member of the Juvenile Court Committee of Chicago, and the Chicago Book and Play Club; on the executive board of Chicago's Round Table of Christians and Jews, the local chapter of the National Con-ference of Christians and Jews. She served, too, as a member of the local Committee for Wilson and helped in his campaign. Although strongly against entering World War I, when the United States finally entered the conflict she aided the war effort and served as chairman of the City War and Leaders Committee.

In 1923 on her first visit to Palestine she renewed her acquaintance with Henrietta Szold for whose work she expressed unbounded admiration, although she personally did not believe in Zionism or a Zionist state. Her inclinations were that Palestine should become a sanctuary for persecuted Jews under adequate protection.

She died on December 7, 1942, 29 years after her husband, having lived a long, happy, and fruitful life.

Hannah Solomon was not only a good mother and wife, a fine cook and able housekeeper, but she managed to take active part in a wide variety of organizational work. She was cultured though not brilliant or highly educated. Thoroughly Americanized, she was nevertheless a committed and loyal Jew. Time, place, and circumstance enabled Mrs. Solomon to earn a small but admirable niche in history. She almost singlehandedly founded the National Council of Jewish Women, the first national Jewish women's organization in the United States and the world, the forerunner of, if not the model for, all subsequent national Jewish women's organizations such as Hadassah, Pioneer Women, Mizrachi Women, National Federation of Temple Sisterhoods, National Women's League of the United Synagogue of America, Women's branch of the Union of Orthodox Jewish Congregations of America, Yeshiva University Women, and others. Her National Council of Jewish Women today is still one of the largest Jewish women's organizations in America, a living monument to her efforts and abilities.

Henrietta Szold

Henrietta Szold, whose long and fruitful life spanned both the nineteenth and twentieth centuries, was probably the greatest Jewess of her generation. She was a woman of achievement, of sweet character and courage, a truly rare combination in any one person. She was meek, humble and unambitious; nevertheless, honor upon honor was thrust upon her in her later life when overdue recognition of her great deeds was accorded her by world Jewry.

Henrietta Szold was born on December 21, 1860 in Baltimore, the eldest of eight daughters of the famous Rabbi Benjamin Szold. Rabbi Szold, born in Hungary but educated in Germany, had arrived in Baltimore in 1859 to lead the Oheb Shalom Congregation. He was a Jewish scholar, a believer in German culture and modern ideas, a man of strong democratic and humanitarian convictions. He lavished upon his brilliant daughter the attention and care in education usually reserved for an only son. She attended the parochial school conducted in the basement of Oheb Shalom, where she learned the elements of Judaism in German, and secular subjects in English, as was the custom among the German-Jewish immigrants. In addition to a further study of German, the language spoken in her home, her father taught her French and Hebrew. Her mother taught Henrietta the "womanly arts" of sewing, dressmaking, cooking, baking, and gardening. The child also aided her mother in running the large and busy rabbinical household and practically brought up the four younger sisters who survived infancy.

At eleven Henrietta attended Grammar School No. 1 and after one year moved on to Western Female High School from which she graduated at sixteen. Her scholastic record at that school was so outstanding that it has not been equalled since. That ended her formal education. That she never went to college was probably due to several factors. In 1877, the year of her graduation, there was a business depression especially in the South where she lived. The only women's college at that time was Vassar located in up-state New York and Henrietta was needed at home to help with the busy household. However, her education continued unabated. Since her girlhood she had served as her father's secretary, and at the same time he had instructed her in the German classics and assigned her intensive reading in general history and philosophy. At their leisurely meals he discussed with Henrietta, who always sat at his side, his development of some sermon or paper which he was researching. The subjects ranged from Biblical poetry and language, to some Jewish historical and religious figure, or touched on some current topic of world affairs. Later Henrietta attended public lectures at the newly established Johns Hopkins University and the Peabody Institute. As a result of these efforts, even without formal higher education, she became, without doubt, the most educated and well-read Jewish woman in the United States.

Upon her graduation from high school she was asked to take over some English classes in that school during the illness of one of the teachers and a year later she was asked to teach English at the Misses Adams' School, a private institution run by impoverished Southern gentlewomen. For the next 15 years she taught French, German, English, algebra, botany and other subjects at Misses Adams'. On Saturday and Sunday morning she taught classes in her father's congregational school, on Saturday afternoons she led a Bible class for adults, and on one of the other afternoons of the week a Jewish history class for adults.

When she was only 20, she became the Baltimore correspondent of the New York Jewish Messenger, an Anglo-Jewish weekly, under the pen name of "Shulamith." Several years later she made similar contributions in the form of letters, to the Jewish Exponent, another Anglo-Jewish weekly, under the pen name of Miriam. Her articles ranged from news of the activities of the Jewish community in Baltimore to observations on current events and biographies of Jewish notables, past and present. These topics were always discussed with vigor and an occasional touch of acerbity. As a result of all her activities, she became an accomplished public speaker and addressed literary clubs and young men's Hebrew associations. Her rare leisure hours were given over to her hobby of botany. Thus, by her early twenties, Henrietta was an accomplished scholar not only in the social sciences and English, but in Judaic subjects and the natural sciences as well.

The most crucial event of the period and one that later had a great influence on Henrietta Szold's life was the vast increase of Russian Jewish immigration. The pogroms in Czarist Russia of the 1880's, the harsh May Laws of 1882 restricting the residences of Jews to crowded ghettos, and, among other restrictions, the denial of their right to property and professions, drove hundreds of thousands of Russian and Polish Jews to the United States. Most came to New York. Some landed in Baltimore. Rabbi Szold, unlike many Jews of a Germanic cultural background, went to their aid and helped them find places to live and work. In this work, he was aided and assisted by his daughter. However, Henrietta realized that the immigrants needed more

than just a home and a menial job; they needed to be
taught English as quickly as possible so that they would be
able to find the best possible kind of employment and not
be exploited as inarticulates and end up in the sweatshops
and slums. Accordingly, Henrietta Szold conceived the idea
of evening classes, where immigrants would be taught English, American history, bookkeeping, dressmaking and
other subjects to enable them to adjust to the cultural and
economic life of America. She found support for her idea
among the members of the Baltimore Hebrew Literary Society, and by 1889, a night school for adults, the first of its
kind in the United States, was opened. From 30 men and
women who came on the first night, it grew by leaps and
bounds, and by 1898 when the school was taken over by the
city, it had instructed more than 5,000 pupils and become
the model for all night schools for immigrants throughout
the country. Although Henrietta's days were full of her
regular teaching and writing, she found time, until 1893, to
act not only as teacher but as superintendent. She handled
the budget and interested many people of means in helping
to fund the school and pay those able to give courses.

But these Russian Jewish immigrants not only took
from Henrietta Szold, they gave her something in return: a
new focus on life, a new dimension, the idea of Zionism.
Among the immigrants were members of the *Hoveve Zion,*
"Lovers of Zion," men and women dedicated to the rees-
tablishment of Israel in its ancient land. They kindled in
Henrietta's heart a passion for the revival of Israel. It was
obvious to her that Jews had no place in Russia, nor were
conditions better for Jews in most of the countries of the
world. She had no answer to the oft-repeated questions of
"Why do they hate us so?" and saw as the only solution to
this age-old problem the implementation of Zionism. In
1897, she joined the newly organized *Hebras Zion,* the
Zionist Association of Baltimore. It was Zionism that ulti-

mately revealed the true greatness of Henrietta Szold.

In 1893 her teaching career came to an end. Although she had never had any pedagogical training, Henrietta had become an outstanding and inspiring teacher. Her guiding principal was "that conveying information is only a subordinate part of the teacher's work" and the true teacher will "confine his attention to those elements that educate the man." She did not leave the educational field, only the classroom, giving expression to her interest in Jewish scholarship. In 1893 she was appointed paid secretary of the editorial board of the Jewish Publication Society on which she had served in an unpaid capacity for five years. Her definition of the purpose of the Jewish Publication Society was "re-interpretation in modern forms and English garb, of the Judaism of all the centuries and all lands, and the demonstration of their essential unity." Her duties comprised criticizing and editing manuscripts, translating (approximately 12 works), compiling, indexing, proofreading, seeing books through the press, and carrying on a ramified correspondence with authors. She held this post until 1915. In 1899 she did most of the work in the publishing of the first *American Jewish Yearbook* and was the sole editor of that annual from 1904 to 1908. She also collaborated in the compilation of *The Jewish Encyclopedia,* writing 15 articles for that monumental work.

To her exacting literary tasks Miss Szold brought not only a superior intellect but an almost perfect memory, wide-ranging Jewish and general knowledge, an admirable English style, an excellent command of Hebrew, German and French, and working knowledge of Yiddish. She was thorough and extremely conscientious; her industry and her ability to work long hours were legendary. Although she was editor of the Jewish Publication Society for nearly 25 years, she never wrote a book of her own. She lavished her considerable literary gifts and talent on the work of others. She edited a condensed translation of Graetz's *History of the Jews* and compiled an index volume for that work. Among her 12 translations were the first four volumes of *Legends of the Jews* by Louis Ginzberg. It is a mark of her modesty that the public knew almost nothing of her work until 1933 when the Jewish Publication Society celebrated its silver jubilee and her accomplishments were publicized.

Her father, whom she had nursed tenderly during many years of severe illness, died in July, 1902. She constituted herself his literary executor and wished to prepare his unfinished manuscripts for publication. Realizing the need for further study, however, she moved with her mother to New York City and enrolled in the Jewish Theological Seminary, the recently developed training school for the Conservative rabbinate, where she took courses in Hebrew, the Talmud, and other Jewish subjects. As the only woman student in the Seminary at the time, Henrietta Szold was permitted to attend only after giving her word that it was not her intention to become a rabbi. This study program was carried on in addition to her heavy work load at the Jewish Publication Society. Soon her walkup flat on West 123 Street opposite the Seminary became a kind of salon or meeting place where professors, students, and other intellectuals gathered, drawn by her personality, the breadth of her scholarship and illuminating conversation.

In New York, Henrietta Szold became more aware of and took greater interest in Zionism. One day in 1907, she was approached by Dr. Judah L. Magnes (who was later to become founder and first president of Hebrew University), the Rabbi of Temple Emanu-El later fired by that congregation for his Zionist views, to aid a new women's Zionist study circle. They were called the "Hadassah Study Circle," a name whose origin remains unexplained. These women, under Henrietta Szold's informal guidance, studied the works of various Zionists such as Moses Hess, Leo Pinsker,

Ahad Ha'am, and Theodore Herzl, and also discussed Jewish affairs and current events. At this point in her life, however, Miss Szold was more interested in and dedicated to Jewish scholarship than she was to Zionism.

It was while she was attending the Seminary in 1903 that Henrietta Szold met a man whom she truly admired and with whom she fell deeply in love. He was Louis Ginzberg, the most brilliant member of the Seminary faculty. In her youth Henrietta had corresponded with many intelligent and eligible young men but none had really caught her fancy. She was one of those women who felt that she could marry only someone more intelligent than herself, someone whom she could respect as a superior intellect. No one came close to those standards until she met Professor Ginzberg who then was 30 years old, 13 years her junior. For five years they worked together on various projects, took long walks together several times a week, and ate supper together several days a week. She became so involved with him that when he went to Europe she cried and became ill and depressed for days, even though they corresponded often and at length. Many of her hours were devoted to translating and editing his scholarly work as well as his lectures, articles, speeches, and other writings; in effect she gave him almost one hundred percent of her life. However, her devotion was not reciprocated. In late 1908, on one of his trips to Europe, Professor Ginzberg became engaged to a young German Jewish girl he had met in synagogue and married her soon after. The pressure of working 16 hours a day, together with this unhappy, unrequited emotional involvement with Ginzberg, resulted in a nervous and physical breakdown. She was now almost 50. While she had impressive and numerous accomplishments to her credit in the educational and scholarly world, her personal life was barren. She who had always dreamed of a family and husband upon whom she could lavish her attentions was now a confirmed spinster. All that was left of her five years with Professor Ginzberg was a veil which he once tied for her during one of their many walks together and a broken heart. It seemed that her life, for all practical purposes, was now over.

Having been granted a six months' leave of absence from the Jewish Publication Society, she took her mother's advice and decided on a long trip to Europe and Palestine. Despite some friendly hints that a visit to Palestine was a sure cure for Zionism, she set sail for the Holy Land on July 30, 1909 with her mother. Although there never was a complete recovery from the Ginzberg affair, the trip did wonders for her. For the first time in her life, Henrietta really appreciated her mother, a practical woman full of common sense and a boundless zest for living.

Contrary to the opinion of her friends, her enthusiasm for Zionism increased during her visit to Palestine, although she was not blind to the disease, the difficulties, the errors and mismanagement of various projects there. What particularly disturbed her, and more especially her mother, was the needless eye disease of trachoma which if untreated blinded the young. Its prevalence prompted her mother to say to Henrietta, "Here is work for you." Henrietta took this remark to heart and came to believe that the future of Judaism was in Palestine. Before leaving the Holy Land she wrote, "If I were twenty years younger I would feel that my field is here." After Palestine, the tour of Venice, Rome, and Florence was anti-climactic.

Returning home in early 1910, she resumed her arduous work schedule at the Jewish Publication Society. In addition, she began speaking to various groups, men, women, Zionists, non-Zionists, about Palestine but most often to groups of women from the Young Women's Hebrew Association, Council of Jewish Women, Hunter College, Barnard College, and Temple sisterhoods. Henrietta Szold, who in 1893 at the World's Fair in Chicago did not join the Council of Jewish Women founded by Hannah Solomon because of her disapproval of their aims toward what we call today "Women's Liberation," now became an advocate of that same philosophy. In practical Zionist work, she became secretary of a committee to sponsor an agricultural experimental station in Palestine to be directed by Aaron Aaronsohn, the son of an early pioneer in Samaria and Palestine's first agricultural scientist who had made some important botanical discoveries. In July of 1910 she was persuaded to accept the honorary (without pay) secretaryship of the Federation of American Zionists in order to clear up an enormous administrative muddle. When she took over, she found that the officers and staff kept irregular hours, strange people came in to use the phone, and contributions went unacknowledged. It took eight months of hard work and long hours to put the Federation's financial affairs in order. Her daily schedule, starting at sunrise, included the American Jewish Historical Society index, the *American Jewish Yearbook,* the Jewish Publication Society, the Agricultural Experimental Station, the Federation of American Zionists, and speaking and lecturing to various women's groups. While others who were supposed to be helping took vacations, she worked on, wryly observing that "they of course must go to Europe, they must go to Atlantic City, but Miss Szold is a fine beast of burden."

In the spring of 1911 she returned to Baltimore for some corrective surgery and recuperated throughout the summer in Maine. She returned to New York and her schedule in the fall.

Early in 1912, her work centered on a plan to establish a women's Zionist organization in the United States. The exact origin of the idea is unclear, whether it was Miss Szold's, that of other women in the Zionist study groups, or even the result of her mother's remark when they were in

Palestine. It is clear, however, that it was Henrietta Szold's enthusiasm, hard work, and dedication that gave fruition to the idea and led to its eventual stupendous success.

A meeting was called for Saturday evening, February 24, 1912, at 8:00 P.M. in the vestry rooms of the old Temple Emanu-El in New York. Some 40 women attended and a society was formed with a twofold program: to establish and maintain a system of district visiting nurses in Palestine and to foster Zionist education in America. Henrietta Szold was elected president as a matter of course. The organization called itself the "Hadassah Chapter of Daughters of Zion," but two years later, at the first convention, the name was changed to just "Hadassah." The reason for the name is lost; some say that it was chosen because the core of the new organization was members of the Hadassah Study Circle, others that the first convention was held around Purim time and Queen Esther's Hebrew name was Hadassah. From that humble beginning Hadassah has grown to some 1,600 branches and about 350,000 members.

At the beginning Henrietta Szold was criticized by the leaders of the Federation of American Zionists for not having affiliated with them and for having thus split American Zionism. They also held out the carrot of greater financial resources. Although Miss Szold and Hadassah were in sore need of additional financing, she had now moved too far in women's rights to become subject to any male dominance. She was able to withstand all the pressures and maintained Hadassah as an autonomous affiliate of the Federation.

In January 1913, following up a contact with Mrs. Nathan Strauss, wife of the noted philanthropist, Henrietta was able to announce that Mrs. Strauss was prepared to pay the travel expenses of a trained nurse to Palestine plus her salary for four months if Hadassah would maintain her thereafter. Hadassah was able to collect not only enough for this project but enough to engage a second nurse and send both to Palestine. In founding and developing Hadassah Miss Szold displayed a multiplicity of talents, combining in her own person the functions of organizer, writer, public speaker, executive, mentor, educator, and leader.

The nurses arrived in Palestine and by May had treated some 10,000 children for trachoma. Meanwhile, in the United States, Miss Szold was organizing public meetings on behalf of this project and by February, 1914, was planning to send a third nurse and, more importantly, with further aid from the Strausses, to establish a training school for nurses which would make it unnecessary to send nurses from America. However, the outbreak of World War I prevented this. In addition, the two nurses there had to return home to the United States. However, Hadassah's work was maintained in Jerusalem by Dr. Berta Kagan and three probationary nurses trained by one of the American nurses.

In 1916 Henrietta's mother died. In that same year Justice Brandeis and Federal Judge Julian W. Mack set up a fund for Henriettz Szold thus enabling her to devote herself entirely to the Zionist cause and the Jewish community without having to work at the Jewish Publication Society. Until then, she had managed several jobs, an amazing feat at her age of 55 but one which could not continue much longer. Judge Mack saw to it that the fund was maintained as long as Miss Szold lived, allowing her to continue on to even greater achievements.

In June of 1916 the World Zionist Organization appealed to American Zionists to send medical help to Palestine where the war had left few doctors and no drugs to cope with the epidemics raging throughout the country. With the backing of the Zionist Organization of America and the Joint Distribution Committee, Hadassah undertook to organize an American Zionist Medical Unit for Palestine. The task of organization and much of the fund-raising for Hadassah's share of the budget fell to Miss Szold who traveled and spoke throughout the country. The Medical Unit set sail for Palestine in June, 1918 and consisted of 44 trained medical persons and 400 tons of equipment. Hospitals were set up in Tiberias, Jerusalem, Jaffa, Haifa, and Safed.

In 1917 came the Balfour Declaration in which the British government promised to establish a national home for the Jewish people in Palestine. Soon after, Jerusalem was taken by British forces under General Edmund Allenby. In 1918 at a national convention in Pittsburgh of the Zionist Organization of America, as the Federation was then renamed, Miss Szold, in order to present a united front of all Zionists, brought Hadassah into the organization becoming Secretary for Education of the Zionist Organization of America. She still remained president of Hadassah which was now six years old, and had five thousand members and over 50 chapters throughout the country.

Henrietta Szold eventually had to follow the American Zionist Medical Unit to Palestine. Administrative and public relations problems of great complexity arose when the Unit tried to carry out its functions in Palestine and its director appealed for help from America. So at 55, and not very strong in health, Henrietta Szold embarked on a new and arduous career as a pioneer in Palestine. She was now about to begin the most significant period of her life and would spend almost all of her remaining 25 years living and working in Palestine.

She arrived early in 1920 intending to stay only two years, and immediately plunged into the maze of problems. The land was ravaged by a recent Arab pogrom aided by the British government. She traveled up and down the country, observed the activities of the Unit, and acquainting herself with the general health situation, studied the needs of the pioneering immigrants. She soon became the director of the Unit, ran the newly established Nurses' Training School, laboratories, and clinics, and directed health work in the Jewish schools. All in all she found the Unit was doing an excellent job. With the aid of another unexpected gift from the generous Nathan Strauss, the Unit was able to survive a very difficult period in 1922 and was expanded, enlarged, and transformed into the Hadassah Medical Organization whose budget was supplied by the Hadassah Women's Organization.

In March of 1923 Henrietta Szold received an overriding summons from America; Rachel, one of her sisters, was mortally ill and if she wished to see her sister alive she had better come at once. She returned to America and resumed the active presidency of a thriving and expanding Hadassah. It now seemed that the rest of her life would be spent in America except for occasional trips to Palestine.

She made several trips overseas, to Palestine in connection with problems at the Medical Unit, and to Europe at the Zionist convention in London to ensure her budget allotment. The Zionist conventions were full of party conflicts and they were unhappy with Hadassah's independence. However, with Henrietta Szold's presence at the convention the money was forthcoming. In 1927 at the Zionist Congress in Basel, despite the opposition of the Labor Zionists, she was elected the first woman member of the Palestine Zionist Executive, a non-party triumvirate, with responsibility for education and health. She resigned as president of Hadassah and made preparations to return to Palestine. Before she left, a testimonial dinner was given in her honor in the Hotel Astor where she was praised by Zionist leaders, rabbis, and distinguished scholars.

Her return to the Holy Land in 1927 coincided with a period of severe economic depression. The educational and medical institutions were in complete disarray. American and German Jews resigned their posts at the Medical Unit and the various Zionist parties had established competing educational and medical systems. It was a tribute to Henrietta's political acumen, integrity, and impartiality that she was able to bring some semblance of order out of these chaotic conditions. She was now 68 years old.

At the Zionist convention held in Zurich in 1929 Henrietta Szold, despite sniping by the Labor Party, was reelected a member of the Executive. Another honor came her way when she was elected a member of the Jewish Agency, an organization interested in Palestine and structured to include Zionists as well as non-Zionists. In 1930 on her return to America, her seventieth birthday was celebrated by Hadassah with great pomp and flourish. The organization was being run very skillfully and competently by a dedicated group of her disciples, and in Palestine the Hadassah Medical Organization was in the capable hands of a Palestinian doctor. But there were setbacks. In Palestine the Labor Party engineered her resignation from the Executive Board. Again it seemed that her work was now at an end.

It therefore came as a surprise and a source of deep satisfaction when in 1931 her most obdurate critic, the Labor Party, nominated and elected her to the *Vaad Leumi,* the executive committee of the new Jewish Community Organization of Palestine (Keneseth Israel) which had been founded under the authority of the Mandatory Government, and she was asked to serve on the executive committee as the member responsible for the health annd education services. Again she did not just sit back and enjoy the honors, but set about consulting all the professional and voluntary workers who had anything of value to impart. Among her accomplishments in this post was the establishment of a bureau for the rehabilitation of juvenile delinquents and the establishment of a training school for social workers. She also gave numerous lectures in order to win public support for modern methods of social service. These activities meant frequent exhausting trips out of Jerusalem despite the hot weather of midsummer and the heavy cold rains of midwinter. Undeterred from her routine even when disturbances such as those of 1936-39 made the roads unsafe for travel, she traveled at first in the convoys, but finding them time consuming, often rode in unescorted vehicles, explaining that at her age there was no time to waste. Miss Szold remained head of the Central Social Service Bureau until 1939 and retained the chairmanship of the local Jerusalem bureau until her death.

In 1933 there was a temporary lull in her usual active life as the British White Paper had stopped immigration. Miss Szold had little to do but read and rest and was planning to return home to America to spend her last years with her family. However, with the rise of Nazi Germany and a relaxation in the British policy, German Jews began arriving in droves. Henrietta Szold led the drive for funds to help settle the new immigrants. The same woman who in America had helped to settle Eastern European Jews whom the Americanized Jews had looked down upon, 50 years later aided the settlement of German Jews in Palestine who were looked upon with disfavor by the already established Eastern European Jews. In both cases Henrietta Szold stood head and shoulders above all this pettiness, true to the authentic Jewish tradition that all Jews are equal.

In that same year, 1933, when Hitler and the Nazis assumed power in Germany, Henrietta Szold embarked on her most memorable project, Youth Aliyah. Recha Freier, the wife of a Berlin rabbi, hit upon the idea of gathering Jewish children who were being denied a future in their country (and who, we since know, would be sent to extermination camps), assorting them into groups, preparing them for a life in Palestine, and arranging for their settlement there. The plan was referred to Miss Szold who dismissed it because there were no funds and no facilities for the children. The settlements themselves were living from hand to mouth and the German refugees were still largely living in the open and were unsettled. However, in April 1933, Recha Freier came to Palestine and personally convinced Henrietta that anything was better than what was in store for those children in Germany. Again one has to marvel at and admire this indomitable woman, aged 73, still open-minded, willing to admit she was hasty in dismissing the idea, and at that age embarking on a difficult task never before attempted.

In typical Henrietta Szold fashion she threw herself wholeheartedly into the new project. She traveled the length and breadth of Palestine seeking suitable settlements willing and able to receive the young people and arranged the necessary entry permits from the British Mandatory Government. She then had to go to Berlin and personally supervise the details of gathering the youths of 15 to 17, teach them Hebrew, and prepare them and their parents for the separation. Last but certainly not least, she had to obtain the necessary funds needed for this momentous project.

On February 17, 1937 the first group of 63 boys and girls arrived in Haifa. Miss Szold came to meet them, having previously supervised the construction of their buildings at the colony of Ain Harod. In her seventy-third year she became for the first time a mother, to thousands of homeless Jewish children. Soon after the first group, more children arrived. Miss Szold tried to make the children as comfortable as possible. She met each arriving group, made countless rounds of inspection to ensure that the children received proper care, and even made every effort to place children from Orthodox homes in Orthodox settlements. No detail or item was too small or bothersome for her. In running the Youth Aliyah Program she was fortunate in having the aid of Hans Beyth (later to be murdered by Arab terrorists), a young and friendly man who had been a successful banker in Germany. In 1935 Miss Szold left the day-to-day running in his capable hands while making fund-raising tours to enable the thousands of youths in Germany and Poland to leave. The chief fund-raiser and principal agency supporting Youth Aliyah became Hadassah, despite the depression in the United States and the fact of Hadassah's commitment to the costly building and maintenance of the new hospital on Mount Scopus whose cornerstone Henrietta Szold laid in 1934. In February, 1936 she returned to Palestine with over $100,000 and had hardly landed when terrible murderous riots erupted, followed by an Arab-led general strike. But the work of Youth Aliyah continued. In the midst of all the riots Miss Szold still traveled to Haifa and met each group personally. By 1945 some 13,000 children had come to Palestine under Youth Aliyah and by 1948 about 30,000 children had been settled under this program.

While 13,000 might sound small next to the 6,000,000 who were killed during the holocaust, our sages teach that one who saves even one life is merited as if he or she had saved a world. Moreover, compared to all the achievements of all the organizations, with all their resources and manpower, this endeavor is outstanding.

On Henrietta Szold's eightieth birthday in 1940, gifts and honors were showered upon her from all over the world. On her eighty-first birthday the *Vaad Leumi* entrusted her with the planning of its fund for child and youth care, and at 83 she arranged and supervised the arrival and rehabilitation of the most remarkable group of Youth Aliyah children. Seven hundred and thirty children were coming from Teheran after an unbelievable wandering of three and a half years from all parts of Poland following the fall of Warsaw in 1939. They had roamed, like packs of hunted animals, through Russia and Persia to Samarkand and Uzbekistan and finally to Pahlevi where the Jewish Agency gathered them and shipped them to Palestine via Teheran. They could not go directly to Palestine because the Iraqi government refused them transit across Iraqi territory, which stretches between Russia and Palestine. They first had to travel to Karachi, then to the Port of Suez, and thence by train to Palestine. When they finally arrived at the Athlit clearance camp in Palestine they looked pathetic beyond words. Many were dressed in remnants of clothing picked up from the garbage dumps of the world. Worse yet, many of them were not only physically ill, and had to be carried from the train, but were mentally and emotionally disturbed as well.

The celebration of Henrietta Szold's eighty-third birthday took place in December and was merged with the tenth anniversary in February of Youth Aliyah. Her first greeting was to Recha Freier, "the author of the idea of transplanting youth from an environment of poisonous hate into an atmosphere of free creative endeavor." Miss Szold, with grace and magnanimity, gave credit where credit was due. Soon after, she fell ill and had to go to the hospital. Even there she was not completely idle. When Dr. Magnes and Chaim Weizmann came to visit her, she tried to reconcile the differences between them which had resulted from a falling out over Magnes's plan for a binational state. On February 12, 1945, aged 84, she died and was buried on the Mount of Olives. Like Moses she saw the promised land of Palestine but did not live to enter the State of Israel.

One does not need any special summing up to know that Henrietta Szold was one of the greatest Jewish women in all of modern Jewish history. She had a brilliant mind which was both orginal and retentive. She was undogmatic, able to concentrate for long stretches of time, conscientious, and an excellent administrator and leader. Though crushed by the lack of fulfillment of her dream of marriage, she managed to overcome her extreme disappointment and go on to even greater achievements. Originator of the idea of night school for immigrants, editor and translator for the Jewish Publication Society, Zionist leader, founder of Hadassah, administrator of the Medical Unit in Palestine, driving force behind Youth Aliyah: any single one of these jobs would have been enough of an accomplishment for one person. That a single individual accomplished all of them is incredible.

Gertrude Stein

Golda Meir

Nelly Sachs   Louise Nevelson

Dorothy Schiff

Rachel

Rebecca Gratz

Ana Pauker

Rahel Varnhagen

Lillian Wald

Ernestine L. Rose

Sarah Schenirer

Hannah G. Solomon

Dona Gracia

Helena Rubinstein

Henrietta Szold

Emma Goldman

Lillian Wald

Lillian Wald, an activist liberal reformer in the early years of this century, was the archetype for all the social workers who followed in her footsteps. Trained as a nurse, she developed the visiting nurses' service, the idea of having nurses in the public schools, settlement houses, the idea of playgrounds open at all times, and, in addition, helped develop preventive medicine programs for the community. That she instituted several of these programs is an indication of just how original, persuasive, and dynamic she really was.

Her parents, Max D. Wald and Minnie Schwartz Wald, had emigrated from Germany after the uprisings of 1848. Immigrants were warmly welcomed at that time and the Schwartz and Wald families quickly established businesses and became quite prosperous. Her father, a dealer in optical goods, traveled extensively on business and moved his family several times before finally settling in Rochester, New York, which was the center of the optical business in the United States. Lillian, born in Cincinnati in 1867, had a happy comfortable childhood, surrounded by her maternal relatives. She was particularly close to her older brother Alfred, and his early death left a deep scar. The oldest of the four children was her sister Julia, who married Charles Barry, a member of the large real estate firm of Ellwanger and Barry. The family hoped that Lillian would make an equally advantageous match, but those hopes were to remain unfulfilled.

For a short time she worked for Bradstreet, obtaining credit ratings of firms in the Rochester area, but the work did not satisfy her. While Lillian was visiting her sister one summer, Julia became ill, and the doctor recommended a trained nurse to look after her. Lillian was sent to bring the nurse to the house. It was her first meeting with a registered nurse, a graduate of the Bellevue School of Nursing, and as a result of the friendship that developed between the two women, Lillian Wald enrolled in the Bellevue School of Nursing. At that time the school admitted only "mature" women of 25 years and over. Lillian, then only 22, lied about her age on the application form and was admitted.

Within a very short time after entering the school, her impulsive urge to help people whom she thought needed it got her into trouble. She heard an alcoholic, who had been left to sober up, crying out that he was starving and needed food. Without obtaining official permission, she opened up the kitchen, prepared the food, and brought it to him herself. She felt that she should not unnecessarily delay doing something that had to be done although she was later gently reprimanded. This trait endured throughout her life and was partly responsible for her subsequent success. Whenever something needed doing, Lillian Wald immediately tackled the job herself.

After graduation from nursing school, she worked for a year at the New York Juvenile Asylum, a grim institution where the children were treated like prisoners although some were just orphans or only in need of shelter. Realizing that as a nurse, her scope was limited and that she could accomplish little, she left and applied to medical school.

However, chance again intervened. Mrs. Solomon Loeb, wife of the wealthy German-Jewish financier and philanthropist, decided to sponsor a class on nursing in order to encourage young immigrant girls to take up the profession. Lillian Wald, with connections to this upper middle class German-Jewish milieu, was asked to teach it and she responded enthusiastically. Many of the girls hardly knew English but were eager to learn. One day, a few weeks after the classes had begun, a small child requested help in looking after her sick mother. Lillian was led through filthy courtyards to a dingy tenement with tiny airless rooms. The mother lay on the dirty floor. Lillian Wald scrubbed and cleaned everything in sight, including the woman and her children. She sent out for clean linens and blankets, made the beds, and fed the whole family. Although no stranger in ministering to poor patients, she had no conception of the abject poverty and conditions in which these immigrants lived.

She approached Mrs. Loeb to sponsor two nurses who would live and work on the Lower East Side and cater to the needs of the people there. In May, 1893, a few weeks after her visit, she was informed that Mrs. Loeb and her son-in-law Jacob Schiff had agreed to support two nurses at a cost of $60.00 each per month; additional funds were available for medicines and food for the sick and needy.

Together with Mary Brewster, a friend from nursing school, Lillian Wald moved into the College Settlement House, a nonsectarian facility, until lodgings could be found. A few months later they moved into three small rooms at the top of a tenement at 27 Jefferson Street. Their parents supplied the furniture, the women the hard work and a few decorative additions, and in a very short time the dingy attic became a warm inviting home. The idea of nurses going out into the tenements and searching out illness was new. As they became known, people began knocking on their door at all hours, knowing that no one in need would ever be turned away. Lillian Wald was also scrupulous in her accounting of monies spent; the smallest items were recorded in detail for her benefactors. In a short while two more nurses joined them and their work was given unofficial sanction by the Board of Health of the City. This small effort was the beginning of what was eventually to blossom into the visiting nurses' service of New York City.

In addition to nursing, the project was enlarged to include education and preventive medicine. Part of their job was to show the immigrants just how much good medicine, nursing, and preventive health care could achieve in brightening their lives and easing their burdens. In addition to caring for the sick, there was the question of convalescence and the importance of good dietary habits. Many of the new immigrants were ignorant of and bewildered by the strange foods in their new country and had to be taught how to use inexpensive nutritious food to its greatest advantage.

This on-the-spot nursing gave Miss Wald greater insight into other disadvantages of poverty. There was the problem of children sent home from school because of various disfiguring infections of the skin and scalp. Another difficulty was that children were often sent to school with infectious diseases which the teachers were ill-equipped to recognize. Lillian Wald approached the Board of Education with a scheme to cope with these problems. A start had been made in 1897 authorizing doctors to work in the schools, and by 1902 medical examinations were required in all grades. Lillian Wald's contribution was the addition of a nursing service to that of the doctors. The nurses' job was to check up on all children sent home because of illness, to certify that the illness was treated, and to report when the child was ready for readmission, in addition to treating all minor ailments in the schools. These additional duties not only expedited treatment, but enabled the doctors to do their work more efficiently.

The three small rooms on Jefferson Street soon became too cramped for the four nurses who worked there. Thanks once again to the generosity of Jacob Schiff, his family and many close friends, a house at 265 Henry Street was purchased to be used as a nurses' settlement. The settlement house was an idea started in England and later transplanted to the United States, whereby educated concerned reformers lived and worked among the poor in order to learn at first hand of their problems. Lillian Wald and the other nurses moved in the summer of 1895, and their permanent home became known the world over as "The House on Henry Street." Three years later, in addition to the original four, another seven nurses were added to the staff and two years later, another eight joined the community. Two lay volunteers, Nina Loeb and Helen McDowell, organized a kindergarten. The backyard of the house was turned into a playground which was kept open at all times for the children of the neighborhood. It was the prototype of the public playgrounds later constructed throughout the city in schools and parks.

Lillian Wald was an excellent judge of character, able to pick efficient hard-working, congenial people to fit into the rapidly expanding community. Common sense, charm, sympathy, and endless hard work were the ingredients of her phenomenal success. She tried to maintain her personal relationships with the people who came for aid, but this became impossible as the activities and work expanded. Due to her sponsorship and influence, many novel ideas that originated in Henry Street were incorporated into the educational system of the City, among them classes for art, music, and drama. The neighborhood playhouse on Grand Street was donated to the settlement in 1915 by Alice and

Irene Lewisohn, firm supporters of Miss Wald's work for many years. Henry Street Playhouse produced performances which often received rave reviews and were frequently sold out.

Lillian Wald was prominent among the reformers who fought against child labor. This was not only a fight against unscrupulous employers but also involved educating the parents themselves. With well meant but misguided intentions, they frequently abetted the situation by encouraging their children to work, rather than accept charity. Many discussions took place around the breakfast table in Henry Street concerning this problem. One suggestion offered was to enlist Federal aid. Such reforms are never achieved overnight and eight years were to pass before the creation of the Children's Bureau in 1908. Miss Wald was also a firm supporter of the unionization of the needle trades, and she served on many commissions set up to examine the working conditions of the new immigrants.

Some of the other causes she ardently supported included the Russian Revolution, Prohibition, and pacifism in World War I. As a well-known public figure and reformer she could hardly avoid controversy and severe criticism, but she survived it all with her reputation and integrity intact.

The Henry Street Settlement sent workers out into all parts of the city. Many of the young people who used it made names for themselves in business, politics and the arts. They, in their turn, supported its work with generous donations.

Lillian Wald herself remained active until 1932, when she was forced to retire because of ill health. She was created president emeritus of the Henry Street Settlement Association and maintained her interest in all its activities up to her death in September, 1940 at the age of 75. She had purchased a home in Westport, Connecticut, in 1917 and had spent short vacations there from time to time. In later years she was to use it more and more as a pleasant retreat from the incessant work in New York City. She spent many months traveling to Europe as the official delegate from the United States at international conferences on social problems and was invited by the Russian government to visit Russia in 1924.

Miss Wald wrote two books about the Settlement, one in 1915 entitled *The House on Henry Street,* and the second in 1933, during her retirement, called *Windows on Henry Street.* Both books do not relate very much of her own life but describe the people whom the Settlement served.

Lillian Wald may be considered among the great social workers of the twentieth century. Although she was not always wise in her political judgments, her humanity, kindness, friendliness, and sympathy endeared her to two generations of immigrants. No social history of the United States can be written without her name figuring prominently.

Emma Goldman

Emma Goldman was the most famous and most influential anarchist in the United States and certainly the most outstanding female anarchist of this century. A brilliant orator and publicist, her nickname "Red Emma" became a household word invoked by parents to frighten their offspring into obedience. In reality, however, she was more of a reformer and social visionary, a fact which her anarchism unfortunately clouded for the public.

The first child of the second marriage of Taube Bienovitch Zadekoff to Abraham Goldman, Emma was born in Kovno, Lithuania, in 1869 in what was called the "Pale of Settlement," a restricted area of Russia in which Jews lived, and which they were not permitted to leave. There were two half-sisters from her mother's first marriage, Lena and Helena, and two younger brothers, Herman and Morris. Unable to earn a satisfactory living, Abraham Goldman vented his anger and frustration almost exclusively on Emma who in self-defense quickly learned to protect herself by clever retorts. Only Helena defended her and offered consolation, Lena disliked Emma intensely while her mother always sided with her husband. When she was 15 her father proposed a match to which she objected vociferously. Her father's reply was to throw the book she was reading into the fire, shouting, "Girls do not have to learn

much. All a Jewish daughter needs to know is how to prepare gefilte fish, cut noodles fine, and give the man plenty
of children." Emma resisted all his efforts at taming her despite beatings and other severe punishments. Nevertheless,
she admired her parents in many ways despite their differences while at the same time, she recognized their faults.

All the Goldman children hated their environment.
Lena was the first to leave home for America, Emma and
Helena following soon after. The rest of the family left for
America a few years later.

Emma's and Helena's arrival in 1886 in the "promised
land" was disheartening. The harassed officials who proces-
sed their papers were rude and surly, as are most bureau-
crats. The two sisters made their way to Rochester where
Lena and her husband had settled. Emma obtained a job in
a corset factory earning $2.50 for a 60-hour week. Learning
quickly, she soon found a better job, earning $4.00 per
week. Here she met Jacob Kersner, a Russian Jew who pro-
fessed an interest in reading and theatre, and a concern for
the poor and downtrodden, the social issues that were dear
to Emma. In 1887, after a four-month courtship, they were
married. Their marriage was a disaster. Not only was Kersner impotent, but he developed a passion for cards. They
were divorced a year later by the same rabbi who had married them. However, under pressure from her parents and
Kersner himself, who threatened to commit suicide, Emma
consented to remarry him. Within a short time, however,
she left him for good, and took the train to New York.

Twenty years old when she arrived in New York City,
Emma was an energetic plumpish 120 pounds and a little
under five feet tall. Highly intelligent, an excellent speaker
and writer, she was drawn to anarchism as an answer to the
contradictions she saw around her. Anarchism naively proclaimed that formal government of any kind is unnecessary
and wrong in principle. Society should consist of indepen-

dent equals, with the family replaced by more universal friendships. The factory owner and employee relationships could be superseded by cooperatives which would exchange goods without profiteering. Some, but not all, anarchists believed violence of any sort may be used to accomplish these aims.

Almost immediately upon her arrival in New York Emma was introduced to Alexander Berkman, an anarchist who became her lifelong friend. Having been taught the finer points of public speaking by Johann Most, her first anarchist mentor, she proved to be an able speaker and debater. She helped organize young girls into unions and was elected to the board of the Anarchist Congress of 1890. Two years later Emma and Berkman decided to take an active part in the Homestead Strike. Henry Clay Frick, head of the Carnegie Steel Corporation, locked out the workers at the plant in Pennsylvania and hired 300 Pinkertons to destroy the union. When they attacked, however, the union men were ready, and in the ensuing shoot-out three Pinkertons and 10 workers were killed.

Berkman and Emma decided to bomb Frick's office. While Berkman tried to perfect a bomb in their apartment, Emma acted as lookout. Luckily their lethal concoction failed, and Berkman was forced to resort to using a pistol. Emma was to remember her night watch with a shudder at the damage that could have been done to innocent people. She never again advocated shooting and bombing to achieve her aims. Because of the added expense of the pistol and a suit of clothes, Emma was unable to accompany Berkman to Pennsylvania. Berkman gained entry to Frick's office, shot Frick twice in the side, and stabbed him repeatedly until overpowered. Frick was seriously wounded but eventually recovered. Frick who had been the villain now became a hero and the deed, in effect, signaled the end of the strike.

Berkman was sentenced to 22 years in prison. Emma was left to continue their work alone and within a year was herself in prison for incitement to riot. In prison Emma assisted the prison doctor, and after her release was persuaded to take a nursing and midwifery course in Vienna, returning to New York in 1896 as a fully qualified nurse-midwife.

For the next 20 years she lectured continuously on behalf of the workers and their unions and for birth control, for which she was sent to prison several times. In the early years, especially in and around New York, Yiddish and German were the languages her audiences preferred, but as her fame spread across the United States, Emma began to speak more and more in English in order to reach a much wider audience. She was constantly harassed by the police who intimidated landlords not to rent her their halls for speeches. In San Diego, Emma and her close friend Ben Reitman were run out of town by self-appointed vigilantes who tarred and thrashed Reitman.

When, in 1901, President McKinley was shot by a disturbed anarchist named Leon Czolgosz, the newspapers immediately proclaimed the murderer to have been incited by Emma Goldman. Despite the hysteria surrounding the assassination and the many attempts to blame her, nothing came of any of the accusations except persecution and ostracism of her family. Anarchism was anathema to the government of the United States, so much so that even those who abhorred anarchists and their theories nevertheless condoned violence against them. Senator Joseph Hawley was quoted by the newspapers after the death of McKinley: "I have an utter abhorrence of anarchy and would give a thousand dollars to get a good shot at an anarchist." Several actually did volunteer to be his target for that large sum.

In 1905 Emma went on tour with a Russian theatrical

company headed by Paul Orlenoff, its famous actor-director. Convinced of his genius, Emma acted as interpreter-manager for the company and took charge of public relations, traveling under the assumed name of Smith as she did not wish to spoil the tour because of her own notoriety. In fact she was so demure and well-behaved that the reporters mistook her for a Russian aristocrat in reduced circumstances. In return, Orlenoff gave a special performance, the proceeds of which were to be used by Emma to start a periodical. Unfortunately, the weather and difficulty with creditors cut the profit down to $250. Nevertheless Emma went ahead with her magazine which she named *Mother Earth*. It was essentially a vehicle for the furtherance of anarchism, rather humorless and not very literary. Its subscribers included many fellow anarchists and of course the police and judges who used it as evidence to put Emma and her friends in jail. Berkman, after his release from prison, edited *Mother Earth* for many years.

Meanwhile the immigration and naturalization service was moving heaven and earth to be rid of Emma Goldman and toward this end in 1908 they revoked the citizenship of Jacob Kersner, her estranged husband. Thus, should Emma travel abroad she could be refused reentry on the grounds that she was an alien. Unwilling to oblige she remained in the United States lecturing on freedom of speech, freedom from censorship, and generally being a nuisance to narrowminded authorities. When Anthony Comstock, the guardian of morals in all printed material shipped through the mails, delivered a talk on obscenity Emma Goldman was there to ask how he could read pornography for 40 years and still remain pure?

Emma became a "militant" pacifist when World War I broke out in 1914. When the United States entered the war in 1917 she and Berkman organized a No Conscription League which led to their arrest. Their devoted friend and lawyer Harry Weinberger pleaded their case before the Supreme Court. Nevertheless, both were convicted and sentenced to two years in prison. Emma was sent to the Federal House of Detention in Jefferson City, Missouri, where she gradually worked her way into the hearts of the unfortunate women who were imprisoned with her. She fought for them fearlessly with the authorities, helped nurse them when they were ill, and tried to mitigate their miseries in many small ways. She arranged for her friends to send food parcels which she shared out and at Christmas she had presents sent in which she distributed to all the inmates. The second year there was enlivened by the arrival of Kate O'Hare, a socialist radical. With her easy access to the newspapers, Kate was able to put into effect many practical prison reforms which Emma had suggested to her.

On Berkman's and Emma's release from prison in 1919, the Justice Department took steps to deport them. This was the period of the Red Scare and the young J. Edgar Hoover was proving his abilities. In all, 60,000 people were deported in an attempt to stamp out anarchism, Bolshevism, and a few other isms as well. Emma Goldman and Alexander Berkman were sent to Ellis Island and from there they were put aboard an old creaking ship called the Buford. The conditions aboard this ship during the Atlantic crossing were so awful and dangerous that the crew was ready to mutiny. To prevent this, the ship had to be accompanied by destroyers on the journey from England to Russia.

Emma had been delighted to hear about the rise of Bolshevism and the Russian Revolution. Lenin, she felt, would give his people all the rights they were denied under capitalism. Emma was in for a rude awakening. When she arrived in Russia she found people freezing and starving in the streets while party stalwarts were given food and good accomodations. Every night men and women were marched off to be shot and anybody who opposed the Bolsheviks was imprisoned. When Emma and others complained to Maxim Gorky, the chief apologist for the regime, he dismissed their complaints with the remark that everything would change when the revolution had accomplished its aims. The climax came in 1921 when the sailors of Kronstadt, who had supported the revolution in 1917, came out on behalf of strikers who demanded better food and more power for the unions. Trotsky, Lenin, and Zinoviev slaughtered 18,000 of the strikers, putting an end to all opposition. Appalled by the brutality of the Bolsheviks, Emma Goldman and Alexander Berkman were determined to leave. They were given passports, but at the same time Lenin sent letters to Sweden and Germany to prevent them from obtaining visas. In spite of numerous difficulties they were finally given permission to enter Sweden for a short stay.

Thereafter, Emma wrote several articles on the Bolshevik myth in *The World,* a newspaper, and also a book about her two years in Russia which was published with 12 chapters accidentally missing. The liberals and radicals in the United States vilified her; the authorities in Berlin, where she went from Sweden, warned her not to criticize the Russians. On her arrival in London, which she went to from Germany, she was befriended by Rebecca West, who although apolitical, introduced her to all the socialist intellectuals of the time: Bertrand Russell, Havelock Ellis, Israel Zangwill, and Harold Laski. However, her denunciation of the Communists was greeted by them with strong protests and they refused to support her. While in England she married James Colton, a Scottish widower in his late 60's who graciously performed this act in order to give Emma a passport and citizenship. During the 1920's Emma toured Canada lecturing on such varied subjects as birth control, the Sacco and Vanzetti miscarriage of justice, and Ibsen and other playwrights. Her friends, Peggy

Guggenheim, Theodore Dreiser, and Edna St. Vincent Millay among others, raised $2,500. so that she could begin writing her autobiography. She settled in St. Tropez, France, with Berkman only a few miles away, and wrote her life story in minute detail, including a list of her aches and pains. Berkman edited sections as they were written, censoring, encouraging, and criticizing at the same time. They argued incessantly, but the final result, *Living My Life*, is a well-written, fascinating account of a life lived with zest, and which was uncompromising in its pursuit of freedom, justice, and the rights of the individual. The book was reviewed in all the major literary magazines and newspapers in England and the United States. The reviewers were not universally in agreement about the merits, but most felt that it was an extremely interesting document. No one could afford to praise it too much since it—and its author—were so controversial.

During the last years of her life Emma had difficulty making ends meet, as her only secure income was a monthly allowance of $30 sent her by her brother Morris starting in 1934. She traveled throughout Europe lecturing on the Nazi menace in Germany and spent 90 days in the United States on a lecture tour which was a failure; the Communists attacked her violently while the liberals and radicals shunned her because of her opposition to Bolshevism.

Alexander Berkman who had cancer committed suicide in 1936, unwilling to face the future as a chronic invalid. Their long association had bolstered Emma's confidence throughout her life. Shortly after this event the Spanish Civil War broke out. Emma tried to rally support against the fascists who were supported by the Nazis, but most of the countries were so busy appeasing the Germans that they did not wish to get involved. With the defeat of the Spanish Loyalists and the ominous signs throughout the rest of

Europe, Emma returned to Canada where she died in May, 1940.

Emma Goldman spent her life in the struggle for her ideals. While she could not possibly achieve them through her efforts many people were made aware of abuses and curtailment of human rights. She was a persuasive speaker and debater, and the United States government considered her much more dangerous than most of her fellow anarchists. Eventually most of the radical causes she fought for became part of the fabric of life in the democratic countries, freedom of the individual, the right to form unions, birth control, and women's rights. She was the first to speak out against the horrors of Communism, Nazism, Fascism, and some of the more blatant abuses of capitalism. It is a pity that in the early days she allied herself with some of the worst abuses of anarchism, the violence and bomb throwing, so that much of her effectiveness was frittered away.

Emma lived her life with gusto, honesty and truthfulness as she perceived it, always willing to help a fellow human in distress. In the final analysis her most enduring monuments are her autobiography, which is an important document for sociologists and historians of the first quarter of the twentieth century, and the influence she has had on social reforms in the free world.

Helena Rubinstein

Helena Rubinstein was a brilliant businesswoman and one of the richest self-made women in history. She singlehandedly established a new business, cosmetics, which is not only one of the top 10 industries in the United States, but stimulated many other entrepreneurs who themselves have created major enterprises around this industry.

Helena Rubinstein deliberately clouded her early origins in mystery because she liked to stimulate news about herself and was perhaps somewhat ashamed of her early life. The eldest of eight daughters, she was born in Cracow, Poland, on December 25, 1872, of supposedly moderately well-to-do parents. As her story goes, Helena attended the University of Cracow and studied medicine briefly in Zurich, Switzerland, where she met a fellow medical student whom her father refused to let her marry. Disappointed, she gave up her studies and shipped out to Australia. To pay for her ticket, her mother sold a piece of jewelry. The reason she decided on Australia was that her mother's brother, a widower lived there with his daughter who was a pen pal of Helena. In her trunk were 12 jars of beauty cream which was to become the foundation of her enormous empire.

Madame (as she preferred to be called) Rubinstein was always hazy about the origin of "creme valaz," the cream with which she came to Australia and first started in business. Madame Rubinstein claimed that a Doctor Lykusky, a Hungarian friend of her mother who had been introduced to her by the Polish actress Jodjeska, gave her this cream.

The true reason for her emigrating we shall never know, but most likely her parents were poor and she hoped to better herself. After a seven-week journey she arrived in Australia and settled in Coleraine, a small town of 2,000 people about 80 miles from Melbourne, in the house of her uncle, Louis Silberfeld, an oculist who also ran a general store and raised a few sheep on the side.

Her story relates that all the people envied her complexion. Encouraged by another pen friend, (she was a tireless letter writer) and aided financially by a loan of 200 pounds from yet another friend whom she met on the boat, she opened a cream and beauty shop in Melbourne. In almost no time at all she amassed a tidy sum of $100,000. By 1908 she had decided to start her business in Europe.

Again, closer to the truth, is that she worked at various jobs, among them that of a waitress, before starting in business. Also, her success was much slower and more difficult than she claimed. However, success did come in time. It was due in large measure to the fact that she was the first cosmetician to realize that dry and oily skins should not be treated with the same products and was the first to offer every client a personal skin analysis with every jar of cream.

After sailing for London in 1908, she was married to Edward Titus (né Morganbesser) an American newspaperman stationed in Melbourne. In London she opened the first modern beauty salon in the Western Hemisphere. It was situated in Mayfair, a 20-room mansion that had once belonged to Robert Arthur Talbot Gascoyne-Cecil, third Marquess of Salisbury, who succeeded Gladstone as Prime Minister. Her business prospered greatly and this European operation began making fabulous profits to add to those from her Australian enterprise. That end of the business was managed by two of her sisters and it was the mark of her way of doing business, for better or for worse, that she never entrusted any major positions in her business empire to any one who was not in some way related to her.

During World War I Madame Rubinstein decided to start operations in the United States, and in February, 1915, she opened a Maison de Beauté at 15 East 49 Street and various beauty salons across the United States. However, in the United States she had formidable competition from an equally brilliant woman dealing in cosmetics, Elizabeth Arden. The two began an intense and much publicized rivalry. However, there was more than enough business for both firms as the fledgling industry expanded.

In 1916 she was separated from her husband. She had borne him two sons while in England, Roy in 1909 and Horace, her favorite, three years later. Two years after the separation, Titus went to France and there opened a bookshop and a publishing house. He began to publish the works of such authors as James Joyce, Ernest Hemingway, D. H. Lawrence, and e. e. cummings. However, Madame Rubinstein, who did not have much interest in anything that did not show immediate profits, cut off his funds and the publishing house failed. Titus also had a talent for real estate, art and sculpture, as well as a flair for advertising, and in all these fields Madame Rubinstein profited greatly from his advice. She divorced him in 1938 and married a Russian prince from Georgia of dubious credentials, 20 years her junior, In spite of the age differential she still outlived him.

In 1928, just before the stock market crash, Madame Rubinstein pulled off a major financial coup. She sold two-thirds of her business to Lehman Brothers for seven and a third million dollars. When the crash came, the stock fell. She began writing letters to the women stockholders pointing out how men, particularly bankers, could not understand the beauty needs of the American woman, thereby ruining the business. Lehman was forced to sell the business back to her for one and a half million dollars.

In addition to her extensive cosmetics empire, Madame Rubinstein had worldwide real estate holdings as well as over one million dollars worth of jewelry and an art collection that was sold after her death for about four million dollars. She was able to make money in virtually any field she touched.

Madame Rubinstein spoke many languages, but none fluently. She was very poor in remembering names and peppered her speech with descriptive Jewish words; *meshuggenah* (slightly batty), *nebbish* (shmo), *macher* (big shot), *nudnik,* (nuisance) are just a few of the expressions she used. These expressions were the full extent of her Jewish commitment. In her career she rarely met any antisemitism. When she did encounter it, however, she fought it in her own inimitable style. In 1941 she was looking for a new apartment for herself in New York. She would only consider an apartment on the top floor and finally found what she wanted; a white elephant, a 30-room triplex on Park Avenue. When she telephoned the agent to rent it, she was told the building was restricted, that Jewish people were not allowed to live there. So Madame Rubinstein did the only thing she could under the circumstances—she bought the entire building!

In 1951 another novel idea occurred to her. What she had done for women, she decided to do for men. Accordingly, she opened one of the first men's boutiques in New York. It was to close one year later; the idea was 20 years premature.

In 1958 Madame Rubinstein went on a world tour for business and pleasure. She stopped off in Israel where she had family, although she did not relish the prospect of meeting them. She decided to build a cosmetics factory in Tel Aviv but in order to get government permission for this project, she had to promise to either build or donate a museum. A large delegation, whom she labeled "beggars" to her handsome Irish confidant, met her when she arrived in Tel Aviv. Ben-Gurion tendered her a state dinner about which she later complained that the food was kosher and bland. The Israelis seemed to her like strangers from another planet. Even Golda Meir, who was delegated to complete the museum-factory deal, somehow irritated her. She finally grudgingly donated about half a million dollars to build the Helena Rubinstein Pavilion in Tel Aviv and gave them only two pictures from her vast collection. She might have given or willed to the museum a marvelous collection at little or no cost to herself through the generosity of United States tax laws, but she did not. In general, she neither donated nor left anything to anyone even though when she died in 1965 her estate was valued at between one hundred and one hundred and thirty million dollars.

Helena Rubinstein was a calculating tycoon with the mentality of a tight-fisted peasant. She gave to virtually no charity and had no feelings for anything Jewish. However, she had vision, inventiveness, and courage, and literally changed the face of every woman in the world. With a negligible knowledge of English, chemistry, or business procedures, she was able to expand a single cream into a cosmetics line of more than 500 items and over one hundred million dollars in sales, found an entirely new industry and stimulate many others. Department stores and drug stores whose greatest income came from cosmetics grew into national chains. Fashion, advertising agencies, magazines, newspapers, radio, and television benefited enormously from the cosmetics industry. In spite of her character failings, Helena Rubinstein must be considered one of the world's greatest business geniuses.

Sarah Schenirer

Sarah Schenirer was born in Cracow, Poland, in 1873 the daughter of a Hassidic merchant, an adherent of the Rabbi of Belz. Her religious education consisted of instruction given by a rabbi who visited the Polish school she attended once or twice a week, supplemented with some popular moralist work in Judeo-German written specifically for women. One could characterize her religious education, however, as virtually non-existent.

Her education, both secular and religious, actually followed the temper of the period. The *Shulhan Arukh* prohibits the teaching of Torah to girls, permitting them only the instruction of religious commandments that apply specifically to them. The Orthodox Jewish community, using a system of logic peculiar to the times, allowed their daughters (but not their sons) to attend and be educated by Christian Polish schools. The sons were given a thorough Jewish education and were completely ignorant of any modern secular studies. The daughters, while well grounded in secular and modern education and studies, were almost completely ignorant of the tenets of the Jewish religion.

When Sarah Schenirer grew to maturity the family fortunes failed and she was obliged to learn a trade to support herself and help her family. Having served her apprentice-ship in sewing and dressmaking, she started a small dressmaking business and soon built up a considerable clientele.

At the outbreak of World War I, Sarah and her family fled to Vienna. There she attended the religious services, lectures, and meetings of Rabbi Dr. Flesch, an adherent of the Rabbi Sampson Raphael Hirsch school of thought which believed in a modern and progressive Judaism which is at the same time completely traditional in spirit. Sarah was greatly influenced by Rabbi Flesch. She attended his study circles regularly and began to read extensively on her own, about Judaism. She was attracted by the ideas of mod-ern German orthodoxy expounded by Rabbi Hirsch and Dr. Hildesheimer. Their writings appealed to her because they were able to depict Jewish life in a way that was con-genial to contemporary Jews. In 1917 she returned to Cracow with vague plans for the religious education of women.

Sarah came to the idea of a religious education for Jewish women for several reasons. The anomaly of the situ-ation whereby boys received only a Jewish education and girls only a Polish one was obvious. Girls, as future mothers would exercise a decisive influence on their children's edu-cation; if Jewish women received only a Polish education their outlook would become Polish rather than Jewish and they would thus be drawn into alien circles. However, there was the problem of what language to use for this teaching. While she admired the Hirsch philosophy which believed in adopting the language of the country, she felt instinctively and correctly that this was not really a viable approach and certainly not feasible in Poland. She decided that Yiddish was the most effective language for her to use. The major-ity of Polish Jewry spoke Yiddish as their mother tongue and it was a specifically Jewish language and so would be an additional factor in keeping the girls within the Jewish fold.

She sought and received moral support for her ideas from the Rebbe of Belz. While the sainted Rebbe was at Marienbad, Sarah Schenirer and her brother sent a note to him asking whether she might educate the women of Israel in the spirit of the Torah. The answer came back, "May the Lord bless your work with success." Afterwards, the Rebbe of Ger and the Hafetz Hayyim, a noted Rabbinic scholar, gave her similar encouragement. This permission was not lightly obtained. Many orthodox men, among them some scholars, were against teaching anything of the Jewish religion to girls. It was not until one great sage noted, with tongue in cheek, that it would be only fair that we teach our Jewish daughters what we must teach any non-Jewish girl who wishes to convert (i.e., laws, rituals, and other essentials of Judaism).

Armed with this permission, Sarah now set out to put her ideas into practice. At first she gave talks to various groups of girls. Sometimes her talks were well received, at other times not. As this method achieved very little, she decided to give up her business of dressmaking and go into teaching full time. Into the small room which had previously been used for her work as dressmaker, she brought a blackboard and some benches. At first she tried to attract adolescents and women of her own age, but they snubbed her efforts. Those girls who had been educated in Polish schools felt at home in Polish and refused to return to orthodoxy. As a result of these disheartening experiences Sarah realized that she would have to concentrate her efforts on young children.

She opened her school for young girls in 1918 with 25 students and called it Beth Jacob (the House of Jacob). The name was chosen because of its instantanous identification with women. This identification came from the Biblical verse

(Ex. 19:3), "Thus shalt thou say to the house of Jacob, and tell the sons of Israel." Rashi, commenting on the verse, quotes the *Mekhilta* (an exposition on the Bible) to the effect that the phrase "the house of Jacob" denotes the women of Israel. Sarah also used this Biblical verse when people sarcastically remarked on the relatively small number of students. In semi-jest she answered that this verse starts with the word "thus," in Hebrew *ko*, the numerical value of which is 25. By the end of the year 80 students were enrolled and the school expanded into a three-room flat. The Agudath Israel of Cracow now undertook to support the school. Sarah Schenirer visited other towns, addressing the Jewish communities and propagating her ideas with great success. The movement soon grew into a whole network of day schools, seminars for training teachers, and evening schools, and spread throughout the major Jewish communities of Europe, America, and Palestine. By 1937, in Poland alone, there were 248 Beth Jacob institutions with an enrollment of over 35,000 girls.

This determined woman launched an educational movement that received the approval of and spread throughout the Orthodox Jewish community. There were several reasons for this phenomenal success, the most important one that it fulfilled a major need of the Jewish community. The character and personality of Sarah Schenirer herself, contributed greatly. Her pupils and everyone who came in contact with her were moved by her piety, sincerity, and integrity. Finally, in what was probably a mixed blessing, she received help from outside organizations. A few years after she had set up her first school, the Agudath Israel World Organization began to sponsor her schools and sent contributions through its local branches. The Keren Hatorah, a fund established by Orthodox German Jews for Torah education, also sent her schools financial support.

At first Sarah Schenirer had to use former pupils as

teachers. Later on, a school for the training of Beth Jacob teachers was founded in Cracow. The erection of this big multi-storied building which housed the teachers' training school was the culmination of everything for which Sarah Schenirer had worked.

In addition to providing the girls with a thorough religious education, the Beth Jacob schools taught the rudiments of secular subjects and some even provided instruction in handicrafts and trained the girls for a livelihood. This aspect of vocational training has been developed and expanded in many of the present-day Beth Jacob schools in Israel. These schools absorb a large number of immigrant girls from Oriental communities who are taught a trade and given the means of earning a livelihood.

Sarah Schenirer lived to see her work expand beyond her most ambitious dreams and to be acclaimed by Orthodox Jewry the world over. She died in 1925 at the relatively early age of 52. She was a modest, pious and sincere person. Though formally uneducated as a Jew, she had a dream to educate Jewish girls in their religion and the will and energy to put her ideas into action and see them through to success. Fortunately for her she did not see the destruction of most of her work in Poland during the Nazi era of World War II. However, her work continues in America and particularly in Israel and plays a vital part in religious education.

She was the first to believe in a combined program of general and religious education for Jewish girls. One may fault her schools in that they did not believe in equal education for girls. The curriculum for the girls is far, far beneath what would be considered satisfactory for boys. This may be due to the fact that the Agudath Israel, an ultra-Orthodox organization became the school's sponsor. As a result, today the Beth Jacob curriculum has fallen behind many of the more modern Orthodox Jewish girls' schools. However, to Sarah Schenirer's credit belongs the idea of educating Jewish women in religious subjects and the establishment of schools for this purpose. The chapter on this subject is still not closed. One can hope that these schools will go much further toward an education equal in content and in all respects to that which the boys receive in their schools or *yeshivot*.

Gertrude Stein

One of the most famous writers and important personalities of the twentieth century was, without question, Gertrude Stein. She is famous no less for her writing, having written more than 40 books, than for being a shrewd and discerning critic and patron of the arts. In fact, it is more the latter, including her friendship with the great literary and artistic personalities of the age, that establishes her place in art and literature.

Gertrude Stein was born on February 3, 1874, in Allegheny, Pennsylvania, the daughter of Daniel and Amelia Keyser Stein, German Jewish immigrants. She was the youngest of the five children born into this middle class family. Shortly after her birth, Daniel Stein had a disagreement with his brother Solomon, who was also his business partner in a wholesale woollen business in Pittsburgh, and as a result, they parted. Daniel went to Vienna where he had some business connections and his family followed shortly after. Daniel's business involved traveling throughout Europe and for a short time his family lived in Paris before returning to the United States in 1878.

Both Daniel and his wife refused to be reconciled with his brother Solomon, nor did they wish to work for him in his substantial banking business. They went on to Baltimore where they stayed for a while with Grandfather Keyser, a kindly and religious man. The family finally settled in East Oakland, California, on a 10-acre property and Daniel Stein became vice-president of a street railway concern.

Throughout Gertrude's early childhood, her father continually made up strict rules of deportment and generally exercised his Prussian notions of discipline. Gertrude and her brother Leo, to whom she was very close, both grew to resent him and for the rest of her life Gertrude described her father as "depressing." She admired and loved her eldest brother Michael and thought of her sister Bertha and brother Simon as simple-minded. She also considered Simon a glutton, as distinguished from a food connoisseur, a distinction which she regarded as crucial, for her love of food was an emotion as profound as any other by which her life was shaped.

Gertrude attended the Sweet School in Oakland and later Oakland High School. She read voraciously everything she could lay her hands on and whatever she was allowed to take out from the Oakland and San Francisco public libraries. With her brother Leo, she continually discussed all sorts of philosophical problems, ideas, and literature. In 1888 Gertrude's mother died of cancer after a long illness, but this did not seem to have any effect on her life.

There were few Jewish families in East Oakland. Daniel Stein occasionally attended synagogue services and the children for a time went to Sunday school. This was to be Gertrude Stein's only contact with Judaism and the Jewish religion. However, she did read the Old Testament and became convinced from her readings, not having anyone around to correct her, that there was no life after death.

Although there never was an instance in her youth of any antisemitism, one trivial incident occurred which obsessed Leo and deeply impressed Gertrude. In school in East Oakland a classmate of Leo's produced a pocket-sized kazoo. Leo, who had already gotten one, also produced his whereupon the boy made the slurring remark, "Oh, those damned Jews always get ahead of us."

Gertrude's father died suddenly in 1891. Michael, nine years older than Gertrude, who had gone to college in the East and then went to work in the same street railway business as his father, took complete charge, and moved the family to San Francisco. The estate was a very modest one but together with Michael's position in the firm there was no immediate threat of poverty hanging over Gertrude. She adored Michael who often took Leo and her to plays and operas. Michael's shrewd management of the estate, his rapid advancement in the street railway business, and investments in property assured Gertrude a modest income for the rest of her life.

In 1892 the family dispersed. Gertrude and her sister went to their mother's sister Fannie Bachrach in Baltimore. Leo went to Harvard, and Simon (who was to die soon) and Michael remained in San Francisco. In 1895 Michael married and his only child, Alan, was born the following year.

In 1893 Gertrude entered Radcliff College. She was described by one of her friends as heavyset, ungainly, and very mannish in her appearance. Her hair was cut short, she was always dressed in black, and her ample figure was never corseted. She wandered through museums, attended dramas, and continued her reading, particularly the works of French psychologists. The prominent interest of her college years, however, was the mind and person of William James. James must have seen some promising aspect in her, for he honored her by admitting her, an undergraduate, to his graduate seminar. Together with Leon Solomons, another student, she published several learned papers in the field of psychology.

After receiving her degree from Radcliff she entered Johns Hopkins Medical School where she remained for two years. Her summer vacations were spent with her brother Leo, who had left Harvard to set himself up as a painter in Europe. These summers were delightful and she longed to enter into this exciting life of Leo and his cosmopolitan friends. Medical school now bored her beyond salvation and her work suffered. In the fourth year she failed her examinations but was offered the chance of making up the work in summer school. The idea of giving up her summers forced her to reassess the idea of a career in medicine. She decided against it and joined her brother in Europe.

At first they toured Italy. Then in August they went to London where their leisure was spent with the Bernard Berensons and their friends, the novelist Israel Zangwill, and the young mathematical genius Bertrand Russell. For a time they settled in London where Gertrude did some extensive reading but this time with a notebook beside her. In the winter she returned to the United States and lived with friends on 100th Street and Riverside Drive in a wooden apartment house called "The White House." Her brother remained in Paris where he rented an apartment at 27 Rue de Fleurus. Gertrude joined him soon after and together they began collecting paintings; Renoirs, Gauguins, Cézannes, Matisses and others, all for relatively small sums. Soon the flat began to assume the atmosphere of a small and crowded museum.

People from everywhere came to see both the paintings and the Steins. Leo was the dominant half, giving lectures to his guests, expounding theories, explaining art, while Gertrude remained silent. However, at night she began to write. Starting at 11:00 she would work until daybreak. For the next 10 or 12 years she refined her ideas of writing and aligned them with those of Cézanne, i.e., to regard nature as something to reshape, or otherwise arrange according to the dictation of one's own feelings.

In 1902 the Michael Steins joined Leo and Gertrude in Paris and also began to buy works of art. Michael and his wife Sarah became notable collectors of Matisse and many other moderns. They also gave the architect, Le Corbusier, one of his first commissions when he built the villa Les Terasses, their home at Garches. Collecting, it seemed, ran in the Stein blood.

Leo and Gertrude Stein were among the first collectors of Pablo Picasso's work. In 1905 while Gertrude was visiting Sargot's, a gallery, Picasso asked her to pose for him and she accepted. That portrait, one of Picasso's most famous paintings, is now in the Metropolitan Museum of Art. Gertrude also sat for the sculptors Jacques Lipchitz and Jo Davidson.

Gertrude Stein was not only one of Picasso's earliest collectors but a very close and lifelong friend. She extended help when he really needed it, when her purchases kept him from starving. She also sponsored him, displayed his paintings in her apartment, and encouraged others to buy his works. In fact, all the Steins have an indisputable place as outstanding patrons and publicists in the history of post-impressionism. Not the least was their influence on Etta and Claribel Cone, daughters of Herman Cone, a German Jew who was the founder of Cone Mills. Their collection of Picassos, Matisses, Cézannes and others, bought from the Steins or on their advice, forms the major part of the collection of the Baltimore Museum of Art.

In 1909 Gertrude Stein was joined by Alice Toklas, the daughter of Polish-Jewish parents who had settled in San Francisco. Alice relieved Gertrude of every onerous activity by assuming all secretarial duties and protecting her from every undesirable and annoying contact. Alice made herself indispensable to Gertrude's comfort. In time they became so close that they called each other by pet names, even in public. Gertrude was "Lovey" while Alice was "Pussy." They were to remain close, in many more ways, for the rest of their lives.

In 1912 there was a falling out between Leo and his sister. She began to assert herself and to outdo him, especially with her writing. Although he was no doubt the more brilliant of the two, he could never really find himself. All his life he analyzed himself but never came to any conclusion. They divided the paintings and he left the apartment to Gertrude and Alice.

The apartment at 27 Rue de Fleurus had assumed the aspect of something between a court and a shrine. It was the international forum for the exchange of gossip, the passing of news, and most important, the sharing of ideas. Gertrude used to sit in her chair by the stove, talking (she had a beautiful voice), listening, and above all being an engaging hostess. Everyone of note in the arts was either a frequent visitor or attended on occasion. Matisse, Picasso, Juan Gris, Francis Picabia, Bertrand Russell, Edith Sitwell, Sherwood Anderson, Ernest Hemingway, F. Scott Fitzgerald, Virgil Thomson, Carl Van Vechten, Thornton Wilder, Alfred North Whitehead are but a few of the greats who were her close friends.

Gertrude Stein's literary achievement is still open to question. Her first work, *Q.E.D.*, completed in 1903, was first published posthumously in 1950 under the title *Things As They Are*. Much of her work found no publisher and so she was published by Gertrude herself. "Melanctha," the last of the three long stories in *Three Lives* appearing in 1909, tells of a love affair between a Negro doctor and a mulatto girl. Gertrude was the first white writer to treat such a theme in a natural way. This stylistic original work is often cited as a minor classic. *The Making of Americans*, written between 1903 and 1911 and published in 1925, was an attempt to parallel in literature cubism, the art form of the period which attempted to reduce images to an assemblage of geometrical shapes. Begun as a saga of a representative family, it was expanded into a history of the human race. It is long, (550,000 words) unpunctuated, repetitious and almost impossible to read. *Tender Buttons*, published in 1914, was a work resembling a verbal collage. Other Stein works included plays, portraits, poems, essays, opera and ballet.

Gertrude rejected traditional literary structures for the sake of authenticity and originality. Some of her ideas about writing are best explained in her own words. In one of her lectures at the University of Chicago a student asked her to explain her most famous line, "A rose is a rose is a rose" (*Georggraphy and Plays*, 1922). She answered, "Now listen! Can't you see that when the language was new as it was with Chaucer and Homer, the poet could use the name of a thing and the thing was really there? He could say 'O moon,' 'O sea,' 'O love' and the moon and the sea and love were really there. And can't you see that after hundreds of years had gone by and thousands of poems had been written, he could call on those words and find that they were just worn out literary words? . . . I think that in that line the rose is red for the first time in English poetry for a hundred years." However, she did not succeed in her aim. Words, unlike music or art, can not be separated from generally accepted meanings.

Although in middle age her works were still largely unpublished, Gertrude Stein was sought after as a savant of the new. She was invited to lecture at Cambridge and Oxford in 1926, and had an influence on Sherwood Anderson and Ernest Hemingway. There are echoes of Stein in the work of Don Marquis and Wallace Stevens.

Surprising as it may seem, most of her fame and reknown to the world at large came from a work written in the usual way. In the *Autobiography of Alice B. Toklas* (1932) she used the name of her friend to write about herself in a communicable, intelligent, and charming style. Of interest as an anecdotal history, rich in personalities and period flavor, the autobiography was a best seller in 1933. It remains one of the best memoirs in American literature.

The book brought her fame, a substantial amount of money for those times, and invitations for a lecture tour. After 30 years, Gertrude returned to America for a triumphant tour in 1934, but when it was completed, she returned again to France.

Other works followed. Her esoteric opera *Four Saints in Three Acts* with music by Virgil Thomson was produced in 1934. A ballet, *A Wedding Bouquet,* choreographed by Frederick Ashton and scored by Lord Gerald Berners, was presented in 1937. Another opera, *The Mother of Us All,* with music by Virgil Thomson was given in 1937. Other written works were *The Geographical History of America* (1936), *Everybody's Autobiography* (1937), *Wars I Have Seen* (1945), and *Brewsie And Willie* (1946). Many of her unpublished manuscripts were deposited in the Yale Library. Yale has published several of her works, among them *Four In America* (1947) and *Mrs. Reynolds* (1952).

Throughout World War II Gertrude Stein lived in seclusion with Alice Toklas in Occupied France, in and near Blignin, where they had summered since the 1920's. At first they thought of leaving as the American consul advised, since as Jews and as nationals of an enemy country they were subject to any indignity, but finally they decided to remain. Their anonymity was protected by their French neighbors, for when the Germans demanded that all the inhabitants be listed, their names were not. As the mayor told Gertrude, "You are obviously too old for life in a concentration camp. You would not survive it, so why should I tell them?"

Strange to relate, Gertrude was a staunch supporter of Pétain and also an admirer of General Franco. Picasso was reported to have said that Gertrude was a fascist at heart, and it disturbed him greatly. "Can you imagine it," Picasso exclaimed, "An American. A Jewess, what's more."

With liberation, Gertrude Stein returned to Paris and resumed her former place as an American fixture in France. She began to hold open house for G.I.s; however she was not to go on for very long. She died on July 27, 1946, of cancer, in the American Hospital at Neuilly-sur-Sein. Although she had been a non-practicing Jew, "special ceremonies" were held at the American Cathedral Church of the Holy Trinity where her body, for unexplained reasons, had remained for several months before burial arrangements were completed. She was finally buried on October 22, 1946, in Père-Lachaise Cemetary in Paris, the resting place of the great French dead.

Alice Toklas lived on until March 7, 1967. In 1958 she joined the Catholic Church. Some of her friends were dismayed but Virgil Thomson understood. It was the Catholic promise of the after-life in which she would certainly meet Gertrude Stein that had prompted her decision. Somehow this intelligent woman had not known that her own Jewish religion also believes in an after-life.

After Alice died Gertrude's pictures were sold for several million dollars and the money given to the estate of her nephew Alan Stein who had died in 1951 and left three children.

Gertrude Stein had a natural craving for recognition. Throughout her life she was determined to be an international figure. Areligious, plain and dowdy, loving comfort and good food, not very rich, she was a person for whom the fulfillment of that dream and desire was not easy to achieve. When she saw that that path did not lie in medicine, she dropped it and accomplished her aims through her art collection and art criticism and, to a lesser extent, through her writing. She did not accomplish her goal of becoming a major figure in the history of literature as her radical ideas of writing were not well received. However, her place in the history of art criticism and as a footnote in the history of literature is assured.

Nelly Sachs

Very few women have won a Nobel Prize. One of these rare exceptions was Nelly Sachs, who shared the Nobel Prize for Literature in 1966 and who was, in addition, the first Jewish woman ever to have won the prize. Just recently in 1977, another Jewish woman was awarded a Nobel Prize, this time for physiology and medecine. Dr. Rosalyn S. Yalow, a nuclear physicist at the Bronx Veterans' Administration Hospital in New York City, won it for her work with radioactive isotopes which can locate minute traces of complex molecules such as hormones in the body tissues. Happily married to a fellow physicist and the mother of two highly motivated research oriented children, a son and daughter, she not only maintains a kosher home but is an excellent cook and hostess as well.

Nelly, or Leone as she was then called, Sachs was born December 10, 1891, in Berlin, Germany, the only child of a rich and prosperous manufacturer who lived in the Tiergartenviertel, one of Berlin's finest neighborhoods. Her family's affluence permitted Nelly the luxury of private tutors and enabled her to study music and dancing. At the age of 17 she began writing poetry, romantic poetry in a traditional rhymed form. At her own request, none of this early work came to be included in any of her collected work.

In 1921 she published an undistinguished volume of her writings entitled *Legenden und Erzaehlungen* (Legends and Stories). This work reflected Christian mysticism in both the world of German Romanticism and the Catholic Middle Ages.

After the Nazis came to power in 1933, Nelly Sachs, like many contemporary assimilated German Jews, discovered her Jewish heritage. She now searched for mystical ideas in the Zohar (a mystical interpretation of the Torah written in Aramaic), and inspiration in her Jewish heritage. It was almost too late. She was trapped in Nazi Germany and seemed destined for the concentration camps. Except for her aged mother, every member of her family was destroyed in the gas chambers of the extermination camps. One by one her friends and neighbors disappeared. In 1940, her own death warrant arrived, an order to report to a "work camp."

Providentially, she was to live. Through the last minute intervention of Selma Lagerlöf, the great Swedish writer and Nobel Prize winner of 1909 with whom Nelly Sachs had corresponded for many years, she and her mother were saved. Prince Eugene of the Swedish Royal House secured a visa for them and in 1940, when virtually no Jew was permitted to leave, both were allowed to emigrate to Sweden. Unfortunately, her benefactress, Selma Lagerlöf, died before her arrival in Stockholm.

Miss Sachs was nearly 50 years old when she reached Stockholm. There she found a two-room apartment on the third floor of a house on the south shore of Lake Malar where she and her mother lived humbly and quietly. She earned a modest living translating Swedish poetry into German. Her mother, to whom she was attached and devoted, died in 1950 at the age of 78.

Throughout the war years Nelly Sachs wrote much of the poetry that was to bring her fame. The motif of the dispossessed, the rejected, and the symbol of the hunter and the hunted, recurred, yet not without hope that "someone will come who will take the ball from the hands of the terrible players." Her poetry abounds in Biblical allusions and in imagery derived from Jewish mysticism, though still in the German romantic tradition. This combination is what makes her poetry at the same time disingenuous yet u-nique. Miss Sachs recognized the reality of evil and accepted the incalculable havoc it wreaks on humanity, but she did not believe in harboring vindictiveness and plotting retalia-tion against the evil-doer. Her magnanimous and forgiving nature was evident in her speech to the younger generation of Germans in October of 1965 when she was awarded the peace prize of the German Book Publishers Association. She said, "In spite of all the horrors of the past, I believe in you . . . let us remember the victims and then let us walk together into the future to seek again a new beginning."

Her poems are mainly composed in free verse using an exquisite German. She is reputed to be the greatest writer of verse in the German language, a "poet's poet" and a careful craftsman comparable with the greatest craftsmen in German literature. Her prize from the German Book Pub-lishers Association states, "Her lyrics and plays are works in the German language at its best."

Her first collection of poems, *In den Wohnungen des Todes* (In the Habitations of Death) contains 50 poems and was published in Berlin in 1947. This work was dedicated to "my dead brothers and sisters." The first poem, *"O die Schornsteine"* (Oh These Chimneys), which speaks of the smoke from the chimneys of the crematoria of the concent-ration camps, sets the mood of the 13 poems which follow. Ten more are grouped under the caption *Gebete für den Toten Brautigam* (Prayers for the Dead Fiancé); 13 are under the heading of *Grabschriften in die Luft Geschrieben* (Epitaphs Written in Air) and 14 in a cycle of *Chöre nach der*

Mitternacht (Choruses After Midnight). Some of these poems were translated under the title of, *O the Chimneys*.

Her second work, *Sternverdunkelung* (Eclipse of the Stars), was published in Amsterdam in 1949. These 55 poems express unquenchable faith in Israel's imperishability and the importance of its mission. Other collections of poems followed: *Und Niemand Weiss Weiter* (Nobody Knows How to Go On) in 1957 and *Flucht und Verwandlung* (Flight and Metamorphosis) in 1959; *Glühende Rätzel* (Glowing Riddles) was published in 1964 and *Späte Gedichte* (Late Poems) in 1965. In 1965 Nelly Sachs made a voice recording of some of her poems in a record entitled *Nelly Sachs liest Gedichte* (Nelly Sachs Reads Her Poems).

She also wrote a number of dramas. Her 14 plays were collected and issued under the title of *Zeichen im Sand* (Signs in the Sand). The most important drama of this collection, the allegorical drama *Eli, Ein Mysterienspeil vom Leiden Israels* (Eli, A Mystery of the Sorrows of Israel), was written in 1943 and published in 1951. It seethes with the horror and mysticism with which Jewish suffering has been etched throughout the centuries. Seventeen loosely connected scenes tell the tragic story of an eight-year-old Polish shepherd boy who lifts his flute toward heaven to call upon heaven's help when his parents are taken away and who is then murdered by a German soldier. A visionary cobbler, Michael, manages to trace the culprit to the next village. The soldier, siezed by remorse, collapses at Michael's feet during their encounter in the forest. The ending denotes a divine justice which has nothing to do with earthly retribution. The story is interwoven with the Jewish legend of the *Lamed Vav Zaddikim* (The Thirty-Six Hidden Saints). Eli was translated into English and has been presented as a radio play and an opera. In addition to *Eli*, some of Nelly Sachs's other dramas are *Nachtwache* (Nightwatch), *Abraham in Salz* (Abraham in Salt), *Der Magische Taenzer* (The Magic Dancer) and *Was ist ein Opfer* (What is a Sacrifice).

Numerous awards honored Nelly Sach's work. Her first public honor was the Literature Prize of the Swedish Poets Association in 1957. Two years later she received the Merit Award of the Federal Association of German Industries, and in 1960 a literary guild in Meersburg, Germany, conferred upon her the Droste-Hulshoff Award. In 1961 she was the first recipient of the Nelly Sachs Preis established in her honor by the city of Dortmund. A special dedication volume about her, entitled *Nelly Sachs zu Ehre,* was published containing articles written by a host of distinguished writers and poets. In 1964 she received the prize of the Börsenverein and a year later the Peace Prize awarded by the German Book Publishers Association. The culmination of her work was the Nobel Prize for Literature for 1966, shared with S. Y. Agnon. Commenting on her award she remarked, "I represent the tragedy of the Jewish people, Agnon represents the State of Israel."

Nelly Sachs's work can best be described in the words of her Nobel Prize presentation: "With moving intensity of feeling she has given voice to the world-wide tragedy of the Jewish people which she has expressed in lyrical laments of painful beauty and in dramatic legends. Her symbolic language body combines an inspired modern idiom with echoes of ancient Biblical poetry. Identifying herself totally with the faith and ritual mysticism of her people, Miss Sachs has created a world of imagery which does not shun the terrible truths of the extermination camps and corpse factories but which at the same time rises above all hatred of the persecutors, merely revealing a genuine sorrow at man's debasement."

In spite of her obvious greatness, Nelly Sachs remains virtually unknown and unread by her own co-religionists. The reason is simple. Her work is in German, a language which, rightly or wrongly, is shunned by the Jewish people.

Had she written in Hebrew or possibly even in English, there is no doubt that her name would have been a household word among Jewry throughout the world and the ages.

Ana Pauker

Ana Pauker's name is almost totally forgotten today, but during the late 1940's and early 1950's, her name was prominent in magazines and newspapers througout the world. Appointed Foreign Minister of Rumania in 1947, Ana Pauker was the first woman to achieve this position in modern history. In addition, as the intellectual leader of the Communist Party in Rumania, her position made her the key strategist of Rumanian Communism.

No one seems to know the exact year of her birth; various dates range between 1890 and 1894. Her father was a butcher, probably also a *shohet* (ritual slaughterer), with the title of rabbi in the small town of Moldavia where she was born. An excellent student at school, her aim was to study medicine, but after a short time in medical school, Ana Rabinsohn became interested in socialism. For a short period, she taught Hebrew at the Temply Coral Synagogue School in Bucharest but was dismissed for teaching the children more about socialism than about Judaism. An activist in socialist and Communist causes, she was arrested in 1918 for assisting in the publication of secret manifestos, and two years later was expelled from Rumania. The two years from 1918 to 1920 which she spent in and out of prison, organizing Communist units and labor unions, reading widely and studying Communist ideology, were important for her future role in the Communist Party of Rumania.

In Switzerland, where she found refuge, Ana Rabinsohn, then in her mid-twenties, met and married Marcel Pauker, a Rumanian student at the Zurich Institute of Technology, a fellow communist and Jew like herself. The son of a publisher, he became a journalist on completion of his engineering studies. Ana Pauker formally joined the Communist Party in 1921 and a year later, upon her return to Rumania, became a member of the Party's Central Committee. Arrested and imprisoned in 1924 when the Communist Party in Rumania was banned, Ana Pauker, upon her release joined her husband Marcel in the United States where he had a position with Amtorg, the Soviet trading agency.

In the late 1920's the Paukers returned to Rumania where she organized anti-fascist and anti-monarchist groups and played a prominent part in the Grivitsa railway shop strike; she was sentenced to the Craiova prison, from which she escaped a short time later. By the early 1930's three children had been born to the Paukers, a son, Vlad and two daughters, Tanya and Marie. However, as an active Communist, completely immersed in party affairs, Ana Pauker had very little time for those children.

In the general anti-red purge in 1935 she was shot in the leg by a policeman; the bullet was never removed and she was sent to prison for six years on a charge of treason.

In 1939 Stalin entered into the notorious Nazi-Soviet pact in which Hitler and Stalin agreed to carve up Poland and the rest of Eastern Europe. The Russian army occupied Bessarabia and in an exchange with the Germans the Russians traded two Rumanian members of Parliament for Ana Pauker, the most prominent Rumanian Communist in German hands. The Russians seem to have made the better bargain as her stay in Russia was fruitful. Many Com-

munist leaders from all over Europe spent time in the
U.S.S.R. during World War II, collaborating and formulat-
ing their plans for a Communist takeover after the war.
Since Rumania fought on the side of the Germans, there
were many Rumanian prisoners of war in Russia. Under
Ana Pauker's leadership and tutelage they were organized
into the Tudor Vladimirescu (a Rumanian hero) division of
the Red Army. When the division, as part of the Russian
Army, marched into Rumania in 1944 Ana Pauker was one
of their leaders and was wearing the uniform of a major.
She was, in fact, a political commissar.

Ana Pauker returned to her country with her three
children but without her husband Marcel. According to various rumors, he had been a Trotskyite when Stalin was
liquidating them and had been purged during the 1930's.
This event led to her reputation for ruthlessness. As one
wit remarked, "this was the greatest possible proof that Ana
Pauker had more interest in ideas than persons." Her rise
to leadership in the Communist Party in Rumania came
swiftly. An excellent speaker, fluent also in French, her
manner on the platform was that of a successful rabble-
rouser. Her booming passionate voice and wide knowledge
of socialist and Communist political theory made her a
formidable political force in the country.

Acting as the spearhead for the takeover of Rumania
by the Communists in 1946, Ana Pauker organized a national congress of anti-fascist women which was supposed to
launch a program for peace, education, and social progress.
She had shrewdly calculated that since the women had just
received the vote they would constitute a formidable force
at the polls. The Communists won. The other parties
claimed that the elections were fraudulent, a charge backed
up by the British government. However, Mrs. Pauker stated
in an interview in the *New York Herald Tribune,* that they
were just trying to explain away their defeat.

By the end of 1947 Ana Pauker was considered the most powerful Communist in Rumania, the only one with direct access to Stalin, ranking politically with Marshal Tito of Yugoslavia and Premier Georgi Dimitroff of Bulgaria. On November 7, 1947 her appointment as Foreign Minister was announced and she was sworn in on the same day that Rumania celebrated the anniversary of the Russian Revolution. She soon completely reorganized the Foreign Office. The old guard was dismissed and Communists were brought into key positions.

Her social life also took a turn for the better. She moved into the fashionable Parcu Filipescu district of Bucharest, bought a lakeside villa at Snagov, and in general lived in a manner befitting her position. The newspapers in the United States remarked on her new wardrobe and chauffeur-driven bullet-proof limousine, but her clothes, although expensive and made to order for her ample figure were very plain and she wore no jewelry. Those who met her always noted her good humor, strong personality, and intellectual and administrative abilities.

Usually after a Communist accession to power there is wide-scale liquidation of any possible enemies. In Rumania there seemed to be less bloodletting than in Yugoslavia, Bulgaria, Poland and Czechoslovakia. There were the usual show trials, but King Michael was allowed to leave the country with his family.

As Foreign Minister, Ana Pauker signed a treaty of mutual assistance with Hungary in January, 1948 and with Czechoslovakia in July 1948, and was also a signatory to the Soviet-controlled Danube Convention which held that only those states with riparian (i.e., Danube River) rights were eligible to participate. As a riparian treaty rather than an international one, it effectively excluded Britain, France, and the United States. Shortly after the close of the convention, Marshal Tito, now at odds with Stalin, accused Ana

Pauker of trying to subvert and overthrow his government. This protest was rejected by her as "slanderous and libelous."

After the establishment of the State of Israel in 1948, the Russians and other Communist states were at first, and in general, favorably inclined toward the Jewish homeland. The new Israeli government appointed the world famous diplomat and artist Reuben Rubin as ambassador to Rumania and stationed recruiters in Bucharest. Throughout 1948 and the early part of 1949, as part of a long-standing but unwritten agreement, about 5,000 Jews were allowed to leave each month, including several members of the Pauker family who now reside in Israel. In March, 1949, however, seven Israelis were imprisoned for organizing emigration and only the intervention of Prime Minister David Ben-Gurion secured their release. The Rumanian Government also attempted to allow only certain emigrants to leave. The Jews demonstrated in Bucharest but were quickly dispersed. There was continuous friction on this subject throughout the year, and the Rumanian ambassador to Israel finally left his post and returned home without even informing his private secretary. Immigration to Israel was halted and in January of 1950 Ben-Gurion denounced Ana Pauker in the following words, "Ana Pauker—the daughter of a rabbi, is preventing her own brethren from returning to the Promised Land." This was the beginning of Jewish persecution in Rumania which continued throughout the 1950's, well after Ana Pauker was out of office.

In 1950, frightened by the apostasy of Marshal Tito and the dangers of nationalism among the satellites, Stalin tightened his control over international Communism. In addition to political reorganization or purges, there was a complete revision of the economic position of Eastern Europe vis-a-vis Russia. Russia's interest was declared to be paramount and all industry and agriculture were shaped to correspond to the needs of the U.S.S.R. As a Rumanian Ana Pauker had attempted to obtain a measure of independence from Russia, but to no avail. Many aging politicians and generals were rounded up, including the Foreign Minister, and charged with the crime of deviationism. In June of 1950 she was expelled from the Politburo because of "active sabotage, anti-Marxist and anti-State activities," and in July, Simon Bughici the ambassador to Moscow, returned to take over her position.

Very little is known of her existence after her fall from power. Two years were spent in various prisons, and after a "nervous breakdown" she was removed to a Russian sanatorium for "treatment." On her return to Bucharest Ana Pauker was placed under house arrest. There were rumors that she would stand trial, but in December, 1954, obviously no threat to the government, a minor post in the Foreign Ministry was found for her. Later on in 1959, known to be in poor health, she was listed as an employee of the Bucharest public library. She lived to see her former protegées in the Foreign Office rise to power in Rumania after the death of Stalin. Her death was reported in the newspapers in June, 1960.

Ana Pauker was a brilliant theorist and indefatigable party stalwart who was determined to make an illustrious career in politics. Like politicians the world over, she was determined to let nothing stand in the way of her chosen calling, neither religion nor money, husband nor children. Ana Pauker was the trail-blazer for all women who have entered politics in the last 30 years. She proved that women can aspire and reach high political office and was the forerunner of such famous figures as Indira Ghandi of India, Golda Meir of Israel, Simone Weil in France, and Margaret Thatcher in England.

Louise Nevelson

Louise Nevelson is among the foremost sculptors working in the United States today, certainly the foremost woman sculptor. She uses many diverse materials in her massive works such as wood, aluminum, and cor-ten steel, and her work is to be found in the major museums of the world.

Born in 1899 in Kiev, Russia, Louise Nevelson was the second of four children. Her father, Isaac Berliawsky, went to the United States in 1902 to establish himself in a lumber business. He settled in Rockland, Maine, a small town with only 20 Jewish families, and his wife and children arrived two years later. Isaac Berliawsky's business prospered. At first his only customers were Jews but gradually everyone bought at his yard. For sundry reasons, Louise felt isolated from the other children at school and had very few social contacts. In second grade her precocious artistic ability was recognized when the children were asked to draw a sunflower; hers was considered the most original. Most of the other academic subjects did not interest her very much and to this day she is a slow reader. However, she was a good athlete and excellent dancer. It was assumed by her family that Louise would be attracted to a career in singing or dancing, or both, but she herself always wanted to be a sculptor, although her fascination with the possibilities of the dance form has lasted throughout the years.

At 19, when Louise Berliawsky was introduced to her future husband, Charles Nevelson met a tall, slim, pretty girl, artistic, athletic, and lively as well. They were married in 1920 and moved to New York where her studies in singing, and dancing continued. Two years later their son Myron, nick-named Mike, was born. The birth of a child led to a crisis in Louise's life; there was a great resentment at being tied down to a baby and a husband. While the arts were appreciated, her husband's family did not think very much of her artistic aspirations. The strains continued for another five years until one night her husband complained about her habit of staying at the Art Students League late at night, not even returning for supper. Her reply was that they could afford maids to give him supper. In 1931 they were divorced. Mike was left with her parents in Maine and Louise Nevelson went to Munich to study with Hans Hoffman.

The Nazis were coming to power in Germany at that time and Hoffman was more concerned with leaving, than with his students. When the Nazis forced the school to close Louise moved to Vienna for a short spell of movie-making before going to Paris. In Paris she visited the Musée de l'Homme, where the African sculptures made a deep impression on her. Those art forms together with American Indian sculpture were to have the deepest influence on her own work. Back in the United States, Louise Nevelson became depressed and frightened that, having turned her back on security and status, success in her new endeavor might be beyond her grasp. As there was nothing in the United States to hold her, she pawned the last of her jewelry and made her way back to Paris. On the journey over she was introduced to Ferdinand Celine who was returning to Europe after having been blacklisted in the movie industry because of his Nazi sympathies. Louise was unaware of and uninterested at that time in European politics so they became close friends. After the Second World War, when they met again, Ferdinand proposed marriage in order to get United States citizenship and of course a work permit. By this time well aware of his political sympathies, she angrily refused, exclaiming that he was worth more to her dead than alive. They never spoke to each other again.

Louise's stay in Paris was quite short because of the unsettled conditions in Europe; the Nazis had taken over in Germany and Franco in Spain. But Louise Nevelson availed herself of the opportunity to study the works of Picasso, whose fiery passion and restlessness appealed to her nature. On her return to New York she continued her studies at the Art Students League under her former mentor, Hans Hoffman. Some of her drawings from this period are in the collection of the Museum of Modern Art. At the same time Diego Rivera invited her to help him work on the vast murals he had undertaken for Rockefeller Center, the Rand School, and the New Workers' School on 14th Street. She devoted all her energies to this work, even though she hated reproducing the small sketches as murals and hated even more the immense amount of research that went into the creation of these social protest paintings. A close friendship developed between the Riveras and Louise Nevelson, who had moved into the same loft building where they lived and worked. Becoming part of the Riveras' social group, she found there were always visitors, diplomats, and friends, and the experience was enlightening.

As a result of exhibiting a piece of sculpture at the AGA Galleries, Louise Nevelson was one of four artists invited to give an exhibition of their work the following year. The critic of the *New York Times* wrote on September 12, 1936, "She uses color as it has never been used before . . . applies it abstractly so to speak, even as though she was working on canvas instead of in the round." This criticism was important because it bolstered her self-confidence and, even at this early date, pinpointed her artistic ability to blur the exact lines where painting and collage end and sculpture begins.

Her existence was nomadic. She never stayed in one place very long and her funds were just enough to make ends meet. Under the Works Progress Administration scheme to help indigent artists she received a teaching position at the Educational Alliance School of Art, however this did not last very long. This period, the late 1930's, saw her slowly maturing as an artist. Most of her work was in clay or plaster models, which were never cast into the permanent medium of bronze. This was beyond her modest means. Most of the pieces were casually discarded or broken up upon her frequent moves from one place to another.

Having decided that she was now ready to be considered an artist of note by the public, Louise Nevelson approached Karl Nierendorf, the most important art dealer in New York in the thirties and early 1940's. He was startled by her forceful approach and agreed to view her works that same day. The result was her first one-man show in September, 1941. It took a couple of weeks of working around the clock to edit and refurbish a suitable group for the exhibition. The reviews were generally favorable. Unfortunately, the Second World War occupied most people and there was neither time nor money for the leisurely acquisition of art. For the next 15 years Louise Nevelson continued to develop her skills, destroying many of her works and saving only those she herself valued. This constant pruning of her work throughout her life has left only those works which in her own estimation were worth preserving. Once, while looking over a retrospective exhibition of her work mounted by the Whitney Museum in 1967, she ordered her close friend to drop one of the pieces he was moving across the room. He promptly obeyed. Louise Nevelson took full responsibility for the "accident."

After an inspiring visit to Mexico in 1956 with her sister Anita, Louise's works took on the quality for which she is famous, namely the sculptural landscapes of painted wood. There were several reasons for the choice of wood: her early childhood experiences with it (her father always brought home pieces from his lumberyard with which Louise played and carved); the heaviness of metal work which required assistance for soldering; and of course the cost of metal. In 1957, observing the lines of a wooden case of liquor, Louise Nevelson decided to assemble various wooden boxes, one on top of the other, just to see what the effect would be. The result was her first "wall." Her "walls" are usually monochromatic, either white, black or gold, and consist of square boxes mounted in rows and stacks resembling a large modular bookcase. Within each of these squares are mounted abstract carvings of wood.

Louise's two major works of the late fifties are "Moon Garden Plus One" and "Sky Cathedrals" two landscape arrangements of abstract wooden pieces. "Dawn's Wedding Feast," a series of wooden sculptures painted white which remind one of the wooden houses of New England, was exhibited at the Museum of Modern Art in 1959. By this time her works had become well known, and museum curators and art collectors were beginning to collect them. In spite of her success today, Louise Nevelson is still angry and bitter at the 30 years when very few people took any notice of her art.

Invited to exhibit at the 1963 Venice Biennale, Louise Nevelson assembled three "environments" from a selection of her works which were being shown throughout Europe; one black, one white, and one gold. She did not win any award that year, as Giacometti took first prize. Represented at the time by Sidney Janis, who represented Rothko, Albers, Pollack, Motherwell, Willem de Kooning, and Kline, Nevelson was the first woman and first American sculptor under contract to him. They quarreled, and subsequently Louise Nevelson found herself owing Sidney Janis $20,000. He claimed that this was the amount spent on mounting a show of her works. He refused to give her back the works until he was paid. She had very little left in her possession because most of her works had already been sold. By selling her home in Spring Street and accepting the help of friends, she paid off the debt, but the anxiety and tension left her so severely depressed, that she contemplated suicide. Fortunately, the Ford Foundation offered her a grant to produce prints at the Tamarind Workshop. The change of atmosphere and the supportive attitude of the staff helped her enormously.

This period marked the beginning of an increased awareness of her Jewish background. Her first work after her return to New York was "Homage, 6,000,000," a huge wall that shows an aggressive use of space. This work is now in the Israel Museum in Jerusalem, an institution for which Louise Nevelson has given her time and effort to raise funds. In 1970 Temple Beth El of Great Neck commissioned one of her walls as a backdrop in the main synagogue. In January, 1977, Louise Nevelson withdrew her promised donation of a $125,000 white wall, "Homage to the Baroque," from the new French art facility, Le Centre National d'Art et Culture Georges Pompidou, in Paris, because of France's release of Arab terrorist Abu Daoud who had planned the massacre of the Israeli athletes at the Munich Olympics in 1972. In addition to her own withdrawal, she urged other artists to boycott this new museum. To Louise Nevelson, the French action evoked "the Hitler era, because it gives to the world another symbol of one person who can get away with terrorist actions."

In the late 1960's and early seventies Louise Nevelson

began, for the first time, to use metals such as cor-ten steel and aluminum for her sculptures. Even in her sixties she was, and still is today, ready to acquire new skills and learn new techniques.

As a result of hardship throughout her life, most of her possessions and prized pieces of work had to be sold. However, she has repurchased the house on Spring Street and refurnished the interior to her taste. It is painted white with a few black areas and is sparsely furnished with steel cabinets; nothing in the house detracts from her preoccupation with the only thing that really interests her, her art. She rarely entertains, is uninterested in food, but has always dressed artistically in striking, outlandish, but feminine-looking clothes, and wears dark glasses so as not to be recognized.

During the Bicentennial year, 1976, Louise Nevelson was among the artists most in demand. A white wood construction of hers was set up in the Federal Courthouse in Philadelphia; a cor-ten steel construction, painted black, is in place on the M.I.T. campus; in addition there are works in Binghamton, New York, Scottsdale, Arizona, and Wichita, Kansas.

In New York City, she was commissioned by St. Peter's Church to design vestments, art, and architectural ornaments. The Pace Gallery on East 57 Street mounted exhibits of many of her works created between the years 1969 and 1975. From the painted wood constructions in black and white to her newer adventurous creations of cor-ten steel and other metals, Louise Nevelson is as completely American as Martha Graham in dance and Aaron Copland in music.

No history of art in the twentieth century could omit the name of Louise Nevelson. Her works have been acquired by the Tate Gallery in London, the Museum of Modern Art both in Paris and New York, the Whitney, the

Jewish Museum, the Israel Museum, and many others. Her main contribution has been to blur and overlap the boundaries between sculpture and painting.

Success and fame have been achieved by hard work, a dogged determination to succeed, and above all a belief in herself and her ability. In spite of hardship and many setbacks, Louise Nevelson has continued, for over 40 years, to learn and improve her artistic skills. At the age of 77 she is still as active as ever.

Dorothy Schiff

Since the invention of printing, Jewish women have been in publishing. Beginning with Estellina Conant who, with her husband, began printing and publishing Hebrew books in 1475 and was one of the earliest printers of Hebrew books in history, to our own day, Jewish women have been prominent as heads of major publishing firms and publishers of important newspapers. Mrs. Katherine Graham, whose father was Jewish, is no doubt the most powerful woman publisher in the United States, controlling not only the important daily, the *Washington Post,* but also the periodical *Newsweek* and radio and television stations, as well as a veritable empire. However, she inherited all this from her father, Eugene Meyer, and, although she is directing the empire capably, she did not really build it. The woman publisher who virtually started from scratch and who had, until its recent sale for thirty million dollars, a popular daily newspaper with a definite and distinct flavor and outlook, is Dorothy Schiff, former publisher and owner of the *New York Post.*

Dorothy Schiff was born in New York City on March 11, 1903, the daughter of Mortimer Schiff and Adele Neustadt, whose father was a partner in the banking form of Hallgarten & Co. Her father was a partner in the investment banking house of Kuhn, Loeb & Co., the firm founded by her grandfather Jacob Henry Schiff, the noted Jewish philanthropist. At first Dorothy was educated at home; then from 1912 to 1920 she attended the Brearley School in Manhattan and also received private instruction in piano, French and German. Her parents had 13 servants and Dorothy Schiff in her early years never traveled in a public vehicle save for the steamship taking her to Europe each year with her parents.

At 17 she entered Bryn Mawr College but did not return after her freshman year. On several occasions she has said that she was asked not to return because her grades were too low. At other times, she claimed that her mother was against her attending college at all and finally agreed to allow her to go for one year.

She was presented to society in 1921. In spite of the fact that her grandfather Jacob Schiff, was a religious man, her parents had little contact with Judaism and she mixed socially only with non-Jews. Not surprisingly, her marriage in 1923 to Richard B. W. Hall, a broker, was solemnized by Bishop Herbert Shipman. Her grandfather was dead by then.

She had two children, Mortimer and Adele from this marriage before she divorced Mr. Hall nine years later. Shortly after, on October 21, 1932, she was married to George Backer. Before this marriage, she asked Rabbi Stephen Wise whether she had to re-convert to Judaism to marry Mr. Backer, a Jew. She was correctly told that it was unnecessary. She had a daughter by him, named Sarah Ann.

In the 1930's Dorothy Schiff began to take part in social welfare activities. She became a member of the Social Service Committee of Bellevue Hospital, helped sponsor a club which provided noonday meals for girls seeking employment in New York, and served as a director on the board of Mount Sinai Hospital and that of the Henry Street

Settlement. She also became a director of the Women's Trade Union League of New York and a member of the Women's City Club and the League of Women Voters. In 1937 she became the Secretary-Treasurer of the New York Joint Committee for the Ratification of the Child Labor Amendment and was appointed by Mayor LaGuardia to the New York City Board of Child Welfare which provided funds for destitute mothers.

Though a nominal Republican by family tradition, she joined the Democratic Party in 1936. Her concern over the Depression led her to an admiration for the New Deal program of President Franklin D. Roosevelt. She became radio chairman of the women's division of the Democratic State Committee in New York. In this capacity she met Franklin D. Roosevelt who was the Democratic nominee for President. From 1936 until 1943 Dorothy Schiff had a close personal relationship with the President which became known many years later in 1976. President Roosevelt even made her buy a piece of land owned by him near his estate at Hyde Park where she built a summer cottage so she would be close by. Although it was just a passing fancy on the President's part, it was an episode of which Dorothy Schiff was very proud. She seemed destined to lead the typical life of a rich socialite of New York.

But this was not to be. One night in 1939, her husband came home and told her that the *New York Post* was going down the drain. The Curtis Publishing Company had sold it to J. David Stern who owned several newspapers including the *Philadelphia Record*. George Backer, who liked to write and who took a lively interest in politics urged his wife to buy it. Dorothy Schiff had inherited a sizable fortune, being the beneficiary with her brother of an estate of about thirty-one million dollars. At first she hesitated, citing the huge debts of the *Post* and the difficulties of restoring it to a break-even position. However, Backer told her that the

Post was New York City's oldest newspaper, having been founded by Alexander Hamilton in 1801. It would be a pity, he argued, to see it disappear. Dorothy Schiff was moved by these arguments and bought a majority of the stock in June, 1939. Some time later she bought the remaining stock and became its sole owner.

Alexander Hamilton founded the newspaper to support Federalist principles against the ideas of Thomas Jefferson. Mrs. Schiff has remarked that naturally she would have been on the side of Jefferson. The *Post* continued after Hamilton's death and established itself as politically independent. During the nineteenth century it supported Jacksonian democracy, labor organizations, the abolition of slavery, and free trade. During the 1930's the *Post* grew more liberal in tone and favored the New Deal. After 1939 Dorothy Schiff continued this liberal policy, growing even more progressive. However, she maintained independence in party politics, often backing a Republican if he favored social legislation.

Dorothy Schiff was told that $200,000 would be enough to get the *Post* out of the red. In fact, it cost many millions. At first George Backer acted as the president, publisher, and editor while his wife stayed home. He was against making the *New York Post,* then a regular-sized newspaper, into a popular paper and turning it into a tabloid. As it continued to lose money, however, she asked him to let her run it. He replied that he did not want to be married to a career woman. Nevertheless, Dorothy Schiff took control in 1942, becoming New York's first woman newspaper publisher. She changed its format to a tabloid and geared its tone to a more popular taste. In 1943 she divorced George Backer and soon after married Theodore Olin Thackrey who had risen from assistant city editor of the *Post* to executive director. In 1943 he was made editor and publisher. He kept these posts until 1949 when a bitter

dispute arose between him and Mrs. Schiff during the pres-
idential election of 1948. Both agreed on opposition to
Harry Truman but disagreed on an alternative. Thackrey
opted for the Progressive candidate, Henry Wallace. Mrs.
Schiff preferred the Republican, Thomas Dewey. Shortly
after the election, in the spring of 1949, Mrs. Schiff resumed complete control of the paper with the announce-
ment that the *Post* would remain liberal democratic rather
than go along with Thackrey's left-wing ideas. She divorced
Thackrey shortly afterward.

The *New York Post* today is New York City's only af-
ternoon paper and has survived the *Sun,* the *World Tele-
gram,* and the *Journal American* and also such morning
newspapers as the *Herald Tribune* and the *Daily Mirror.* It
has a circulation of about 500,000 and a staff of about
1,000 and is financially either breaking even or slightly pro-
fitable. Philosophically Mrs. Schiff is against subsidies for
any newspaper and is convinced that a publication must
make its own way. While its readership used to be from the
Bronx and Brooklyn, today it is mostly from the upper east
side and the financial district, due perhaps to its coverage
of the Wall Street closings. The *Post* advocates unionism
and social reform programs and champions the causes of
civil rights and civil liberties. It can be classified as left-wing
democratic. A tabloid, it caters to popular taste and features
crime, gossip, and sports. Mrs. Schiff generally left the
day-to-day management to others but made all major decisions herself. She decided on political endorsements, which
columnists to hire or keep, and the trend and tone of its
feature articles. She claims, with justification, that she has
popular taste and so is a good guinea pig as to what the
general populace prefers. For several years she wrote her
own regular column, but gave it up because it consumed
too much of her time. All financial decisions were hers
alone. During the 1962-63 New York newspaper strike she

broke the united front of the publishers by starting to publish after an 86-day shutdown. She risked financial ruin by a possible advertisers' boycott but fortunately for her nothing happened. In general she took an independent line in labor negotiations, often striving for better deals from the various powerful newspaper unions. She did not always succeed. Whether the *New York Post* will survive under its new management is a moot question. That it has until now is to her credit.

Dorothy Schiff has very little to do with Israel or anything Jewish. In her early youth she once asked Henrietta Szold, founder of Hadassah, if perhaps she could go to Palestine to help. When asked what she could do, she answered that she could sew. Miss Szold then politely answered that perhaps it would be better if she stayed in America. Frightened and even terrified of flying (she hates automobiles and elevators also), she never visited Israel. However, in the 1950's she met Rudolf G. Sonneborn, the noted Zionist, whom she married in 1953 (and separated from in 1965). Having great confidence in him she flew with him to Israel. Afraid to fly back by herself, she waited two months until he was ready and then returned with him. She did not think much of Israel then and there is no indication of any change of heart on her part today.

As she has characterized herself, Mrs. Schiff has no special intellectual talents and very little formal education. She has almost no religious feeling or loyalty. Although she inherited a substantial fortune, her life could easily have slipped into one of boredom, frustration, and despondency, had she not made the most of her one opportunity to escape all this and create an interesting and useful life for herself, by securing a place, albeit small, in the history of newspaper publishing. She could easily have scrapped the *Post* after its disastrous early years following her purchase. She persevered, took charge, and turned it around. She has accomplished as much as anyone else could possibly have done in this situation. The driving force behind this success is due in no small part to her family tradition, particularly that of her grandfather, not to live a useless life.

Rosalind Franklin

In 1968 a book entitled *The Double Helix* was published. Its author was James D. Watson, one of the three men awarded the Nobel Prize for unraveling the molecular structure of deoxyribonucleic acid, known more familiarly as DNA. The book was a smashing success and generated much speculation since it described in an exciting breezy style how Watson and his colleagues went about their research. One of the people to whom he pays tribute in the book, although in a rather backhanded way, is Rosalind Franklin, who might have been one of the Nobel Prize winners but for her untimely death from cancer in April, 1958. Although Professor Watson treats Rosalind Franklin cavalierly, the lasting impression of this book is that Miss Franklin was a first-rate, meticulous scientist moving inexorably to the top of her chosen profession. Without her beautiful X-ray photographs of DNA, Crick and Watson's hypothesis could not have been confirmed as early as it was and the Nobel Prize might have gone to someone else.

Rosalind Franklin was born July 25, 1920, in London, the daughter of Ellis Franklin and Muriel Waley Franklin, members of a distinguished Anglo-Jewish family. Through her mother's family, the Waleys, she was related to Sir Moses Montefiore, the most distinguished Jewish philanthropist of the 19th century. Jacob Waley, founder of the

Jewish Board of Guardians, married Julia Salomon, a niece
of Moses Montefiore; he was Muriel Waley Franklin's
grandfather. Ellis Franklin belonged to a distinguished
Jewish banking family closely allied to what in England has
become known as the "cousinhood." This is a group of families who, over several generations, have intermarried with
each other and whose names are well known in Anglo-
Jewry; Goldsmid, Mocatta, Salomon, Montefiore, Samuel
(Herbert Samuel was a great great-uncle of Rosalind),
Franklin, Cohen, Montagu, and Waley. Thus Rosalind
Franklin was distantly connected to all the most socially dis-
tinguished families of the Jewish community in England.

Both her father and mother were deeply immersed in
Anglo-Jewish affairs. It was taken for granted that
Rosalind, the second of five children, three boys and two
girls, would follow her parents' inclinations and develop an
interest in communal service. For many years Rosalind was
the only girl (her sister, eight years younger, was born in 1928),
and as she was not a robust child she considered herself
at a disadvantage in comparison to her three brothers. As a
consequence, she always felt that her sex was more a hind-
rance to her than a help. All her life she had to fight for
recognition, even from her closest kin; it is therefore not
surprising that at times she became enraged.

Like many other members of her family, Rosalind was
sent to St. Paul's Girls' School, considered one of the finest
schools in London, England. Although many socially prominent girls have been educated there, the emphasis was
then, and still is, on solid academic achievement. There
was an unspoken expectation that all graduates would, as a
matter of course, continue on to a university degree, a rarity
among women at that time in England. At 15, the students
were required to make decisions affecting their future
choice of careers by specializing in either arts or science.
Rosalind Franklin chose science and at 17, the usual age,

elected chemistry as her specialty, the subject she would continue to study at college. Her father opposed her career choice, but she overcame his objections and won an exhibition to Newnham College, Cambridge University. An exhibition is a reward for scholastic excellence and this signified that even in St. Paul's Girls' School, an elite educational institution, Rosalind Franklin was a top student.

She graduated from Newnham in 1941 and was immediately granted a research scholarship under Ronald G. W. Norrish, who received the Nobel Prize for chemistry in 1967. There was constant friction between them. Norrish viewed her as an advocate of women's liberation; she just wanted the same recognition that was awarded to male colleagues. At about the same time Rosalind Franklin met Adrienne Weil, a French refugee who had been awarded a research fellowship for the duration of the Second World War. She had fled from France with her young daughter on the last boat out of Bordeaux before the Germans occupied the city. This charming and vivacious French Jewess who later gained recognition for her work in metallurgy and was until recently a contractual engineer for arms and construction in the French Navy, taught Rosalind French. It was through her intervention that Rosalind became an X-ray crystallographer.

Deeply dissatisfied with her work at Cambridge, Rosalind obtained a position with the Coal Utilization Research Association. She had joined a group of bright young physicists straight out of college who were working on the structure of carbons. During her four years at the Coal Research Association, she published five papers, the results of her painstaking research on the microstructure of coal.

Her colleagues, the work, and her surroundings were very pleasant and she, in turn, was liked and respected. Though these four years did give her assurance and self-confidence, she wished to explore new fields.

After Adrienne Weil returned to France, Rosalind continued to correspond with her, and it was through her that Rosalind Franklin obtained a position at the Central Laboratory of Chemical Sciences in Paris. There, under Jacques Mering, she was taught the latest methods of X-ray diffraction, a means of analyzing the spectra of crystalline substances, and its application to the structure of coal. Her French, which was good when she arrived, rapidly became fluent. She adored Paris, and made many lasting friendships during her stay there.

Her line of research was new and fascinating. Professor Mēring proved a brilliant teacher and Rosalind an apt pupil and researcher. Professor J. D. Bernal said of her, "She discovered in a series of beautifully executed researches the fundamental distinction between carbons that turned on heating, into graphite, and those that did not." Further she related this difference to the chemical constitution of the molecules from which the carbon was made." Rosalind became a recognized authority in industrial physico-chemistry and her work formed the basis for further research which proved to have important applications to industry. The uses of crystallography were not only rapidly expanding the study of metals and minerals, but were being applied to the study of molecular biology as well. However, there was no future for a foreign researcher in Paris and no possibility of further advancement at the Central Laboratory.

Reluctantly, Rosalind was forced to return to London. She was, however, fortunate in obtaining a post at King's College, London University. Through an acquaintance, she was introduced to Professor John Randall and won a fellowship at the King's College Medical Research Council Biophysics Unit. The understanding at King's was that she would set up and run an X-ray diffraction unit and the techniques would be used to study the structure of DNA. Until she arrived, the research into DNA was carried out by

Maurice Wilkins and Randall, with Raymond Gosling, a research student working under Wilkins. Gosling was transferred to Rosalind Franklin like a piece of furniture. They worked well together, his amiable temperament a good foil for her more combative nature. Her method of teaching was to present the arguments for her position, fully expecting counter-arguments in return. Maurice Wilkins, however, abhorred this method and it was one of the reasons he and Franklin never got along together.

In addition, Rosalind Franklin had an unenviable position at King's, since not only was she the only woman in her department but the only Jew as well. One can imagine the atmosphere she had to contend with. The common room was for men only, and since this was the place where fruitful scientific discussions often took place, her exclusion affected her work somewhat. As late as 1971, 18 years after she left King's, it was known that Wilkins had never accepted a female doctoral candidate under his direction.

Right from the start there was friction between Franklin and Wilkins. Wilkins was having difficulty hydrating DNA and Rosalind was able to suggest a simple chemical method for producing the hydrated B-form. As a result, she viewed him as something less than a genius, while he subsequently minimized her suggestion. He always felt at a disadvantage in his dealings with her and because of this was quite indiscreet not only about his own research but about hers and the other projects going on in the department. He always pined for sympathy from Watson, who willingly gave it in return for the vital information about the progress of DNA at King's. Watson walked into Rosalind Franklin's lab one day and riled her so, that she almost assaulted him. This was his way of making her appear unfeminine. His book gives the impression that he spent more time snooping around trying to get information from others than doing his own research.

For the greater part of 1951, Rosalind Franklin was assembling the apparatus to start her research, but by November she was well into her work and was producing much better results by hydration of DNA and the use of X-ray diffraction techniques than anybody had hitherto produced. Between 1951 and 1953 she showed that there were two forms of DNA, a crystalline A-form and a wet para-crystalline B-form, and she suggested that the patterns were consistent with a helical structure. She discovered the parameters of the cell unit and correctly maintained that the phosphates were on the outside of the helices. She also exposed the errors of Crick and Watson's initial model of DNA.

Without her knowledge (her permission was never sought), Crick and Watson had her research data X-ray photographs, given them by Max Perutz of the Cavendish Laboratory in Cambridge. In order to qualify for government grants, King's College had had to give a presentation of the research that was in progress to the Medical Research Council, of which Max Perutz was a member. Franklin and Gosling produced a summary of their work and Perutz gave the data to Crick and Watson. In addition, Wilkins himself had at various times also given her results to Watson.

Rosalind Franklin was off on a tangent in her research on the structure of DNA, but there is no doubt that she was quite close to solving the riddle. When Crick and Watson published the final results of their model, she immediately recognized it as correct, without any argument against it, as there was when they had presented their incorrect version. When the DNA article first appeared in *Nature*, April 25, 1953, Franklin and Gosling published a supporting paper at the same time as Wilkins did. In view of her ready acceptance of the results, it was incorrect of Watson to speak of her attitude as being "antihelical." This appears to be one more attempt to prove that she could never have produced the right answer.

During the latter part of 1952 and the early part of 1953, Rosalind Franklin was making plans to leave King's where the atmosphere, for her at any rate, was so uninviting. She had been offered a position at Birkbeck College under Professor J. D. Bernal. There she was given her own little research team and she took up the study of tobacco mosaic virus, known more popularly as TMV, one of the most thoroughly studied plant viruses. Almost immediately, using X-ray diffraction techniques, she was able to make notable advances. As described by Bernal, "She first verified and refined Watson's spiral hypotheses for the structure of the virus, and then made her greatest contribution in locating the infective element of the virus particle . . ."

When she left Kings for Birkbeck, one of the restrictions imposed upon her was that there was to be no work or discussion about DNA, not even with Gosling until he had his degree. This limitation was a little ridiculous since most of the vital information had already been handed out. However, Franklin and Gosling did meet frequently and several joint papers were published. She was becoming very well known in her field, a recognized authority on the structure of coal, and she read papers at conferences in Belgium, France, and the United States.

At Birkbeck College, Rosalind Franklin was happy. Bernal was noted for his tolerance of women and his strong attachment to Communism. A great crystallographer, he had been studying the TMV for many years. Rosalind Franklin treated his political views with some humor and complete detachment even through the intense furor of the 1956 Hungarian uprising. From 1954 on, she collaborated closely with Aaron Klug, a young South African, until her untimely death four years later. She was recognized as one of the select band of pioneers who were unraveling the structure of nucleo-proteins in relation to virus diseases and genetics. The Royal Society invited her to mount an exhibition at the World's Fair in Brussels, at which she reproduced the structure of the TMV.

It was also in 1956 that she discovered that she had an incurable cancer. Nevertheless, in spite of several operations and severe pain, she continued working until shortly before she died. Few people outside her immediate family and a few very close friends were aware of her condition; she could not bear pity or sympathy and continued to live as normally as possible, making plans for travel and lectures.

It is a great pity that Rosalind Franklin achieved fame, outside academia, in a book that denigrates her character and ability. Perhaps the author of *The Double Helix* sought to justify his dubious behavior, scaling her down to lab-assistant size by using the name "Rosy" throughout the book. Franklin was much more the image of the dedicated scientist working with skill and precision, than was Watson flitting around trying to find out what everyone else was doing, or even Wilkins, constantly bemoaning his fate in having a female colleague and claiming that he was unable to work because of her.

Of course she was angry, she had every right to be. An able and talented researcher, she fought for her due and thoroughly earned the praise so grudgingly given her. As Professor Bernal so aptly summed up in writing of her, "Her life is an example of single-minded devotion to scientific research." There is no question that within a few years, had death not intervened, she would have been at the top of her profession.

Golda Meir

This book begins with the first woman head of state, Queen Salome Alexandra, and ends with another, a prime minister, probably the best known and most admired Jewish woman of our times, Golda Meir. There is a striking similarity between these two women who are separated by a span of 2,000 years: they were both heads of state of an independent Israel during a period of prosperity and both became leaders at a relatively advanced age, after a lifetime steeped in politics, Shalom Zion at 67 and Golda Meir at 71.

Golda Meir today projects the image of a simple grandmother, full of years and wisdom, who was accidentally catapulted into the seat of power when all she ever wanted was to enjoy the company of her children and grandchildren. Nothing is further from the truth. Like all successful politicians, she has a strong will and had labored many years, working her way up through the ranks of the Histadrut and Zionist Labor Party, the Mapai, before achieving cabinet rank and reaching the summit of her career, Prime Minister of the State of Israel. Fluency in several languages, an appealing simplicity, a moving manner of delivery, and a willingness to work at any political task no matter how inconvenient and unpleasant enabled her to become a major figure among the founders of the

Jewish state, first as fund-raiser, later as ambassador, and then as foreign minister.

Golda Meir became prime minister in March, 1969, following the sudden death of Levi Eshkol. She had lived in semi-retirement for a few years but had held the position of Secretary of the Mapai Party. She served for five years, undoubtedly the best five years in Israel's recent history, before being forced to resign as a result of the depression and bitterness following the Yom Kippur War of September, 1973. Although the Israelis were well on their way to a stunning victory when the ceasefire was forced upon them, the nature of the early reverses and general unpreparedness led to a hunt for scapegoats. The lot fell mainly on Moshe Dayan and to a lesser extent, on Golda Meir. Nevertheless, because of the prosperity that existed during the period of her premiership, she was an extremely popular and respected figure and remains, even today in retirement, the epitome of the successful woman in public life.

A "founding father" and signatory to the Declaration of Independence of the State of Israel in 1948, it is hardly surprising that Mrs. Meir should have been influenced by Zionist ideas from a very early age. Born in Kiev, Russia, in 1898, Golda Mabovich was the second of three surviving sisters of a poverty-stricken family. Her father, in search of work and money to support his family, left for the United States. While he was away, Sheyna, her eldest sister, senior by several years and a dedicated Zionist, held clandestine meetings in their home on Saturday mornings while her mother was at the synagogue. From her niche above the stove, Golda was a willing and eager convert to the philosophical and political ideas that were being discussed. Mrs. Mabovich, unable and unwilling to put an end to her daughter's reckless and, in Czarist Russia illegal activities, decided that her family would be much safer in the United States. They arrived in 1906 and settled in Milwaukee where Mr. Mabovich held a job as a carpenter and was an active member of his union.

In the United States, Sheyna, now married to her childhood sweetheart and fellow Zionist who had followed her to America, continued her Zionist activities. Golda was strongly influenced by her older sister and herself became an even more ardent Zionist. Strong-willed even as a teenager, Golda also had a desire for advanced education. When her parents refused to allow her to continue in school, she ran away from home. She returned to her parents only on condition that she be allowed to continue past high school to teacher training courses. However, labor Zionism remained the abiding avocation throughout her youth. She attended meetings, spoke on street corners, and met all the more prominent Zionists who stopped over in Milwaukee. As a result of their daughters' interest, Golda's parents also became Zionists and gave food and lodging to many of the Zionists who happened to pass through.

As a teenager she met Morris Myerson, a mild-mannered, good-natured artistic intellectual, at a meeting held in her sister's home. They fell in love but she agreed to marry him only on condition that they settle in Palestine. The marriage in 1917 was performed at her mother's insistence by a rabbi under a *chupa* (bridal canopy) and in 1921 the Myersons sailed for Palestine together with Golda's sister Sheyna and Sheyna's children. Their arrival in the blazing heat of summer was an unforgettable nightmare.

The Myersons applied for admission to Kibbutz Merhavia and were accepted because they were in possession of a fine phonograph and a plentiful supply of classical music records. Morris, an artistic and gentle person, was unable to face the bare, rugged existence of the Kibbutz and became ill. He and Golda returned to Tel Aviv and later moved to Jerusalem where Morris had a job with Solel Boneh, the Mapai construction firm, and where their two children Menachem and Sarah were born. Morris Myerson was rarely paid his wages and the family lived on the edge of starvation during these years. The frail bonds of their marriage became frayed. Golda Myerson was offered, and she accepted a job in the Histadrut, the Labor Zionist organization, as secretary of the Women's Labor Council. Thus began her long journey to the top. It was a full-time job which involved traveling and being away from home for varying periods, and it brought to an end her marriage and career as a full-time mother. The demands of her work took precedence over those of her children, despite her daughter's frequent illnesses.

Golda Myerson rose through the ranks of the Histadrut and became a noted leader of Zionism. An accomplished speaker and fund-raiser, she spent many months in the United States and England on speaking tours. When the British arrested the male Zionist leaders because they were trying to smuggle refugees from Nazism into Palestine, Golda Myerson, as acting head of the Jewish Agency, became their spokesman and the Agency's negotiator with the British until the end of the Mandate and the establishment of the State of Israel in 1948.

David Ben-Gurion, Israel's first Prime Minister, appointed her ambassador to Russia in 1948. While in Moscow, she witnessed the first spontaneous and enthusiastic outburst of Russian Jews for the new State. When she attended the Moscow Synagogue on Rosh Hashanah, the Jewish New Year, many thousands of Jews disobeyed veiled Communist threats and crowded the streets outside the synagogue just to touch her and wish her well. In retaliation, Stalin closed down the Yiddish newspapers and several Jewish organizations which had existed until then as Communist puppets and arrested Molotov's wife who had spoken to Golda in Yiddish at a diplomatic reception.

After Israel's first elections in 1949, Golda Myerson became Minister of Labor in Ben-Gurion's cabinet. She changed her name to Meir after her appointment as Foreign Minister in 1956, a position she held until 1965 when she became Secretary of Mapai.

Today Mrs. Meir lives in Tel Aviv in a two-family house shared by her son Menachem, a musician, his wife Aya, and their children. Her daughter Sarah, whom she visits frequently, lives with her husband, Zechariah, a Yemenite Jew, and their children in Kibbutz Revivim in the Negev. Although ostensibly living in retirement, she is still involved with politics and often travels abroad, as her country's unofficial ambassador and fund-raiser.

Golda Meir is popularly considered the greatest woman in Jewish history. Her Zionist idealism, born in the ghetto, developed in the United States and sustained and practiced in the Holy Land, confirms Golda Meir as one of the heroic founders of the State of Israel. Her political and oratorical abilities enabled her to become Foreign Minister and later Prime Minister. All these accomplishements have firmly established her, not only as a historical figure but also as a legend in her own lifetime.

Selected Bibliography

1. QUEEN SALOME ALEXANDRA

Halevy, Isaac. *Dorot Harischonim* (Hebrew), Vol. 1, part 3. Berlin, 1922, pp. 503-546.

Josephus. *The Jewish War*, Book 1, Chapters III-IV.

———, *Antiquities of the Jews*, Book 13, Chapters XII-XVI.

Klausner, Joseph. *History of the Period of the Second Temple* (Hebrew). Jerusalem, 1950, pp. 142-145; 165-178.

Zeitlin, Solomon. *The Rise and Fall of the Judean State*, Vol. I. Philadelphia, 1962, pp. 317-342.

2. BERURIAH

Kaplan, Zvi. "Berurah," *Encyclopaedia Judaica*, Vol. IV. Jerusalem, 1971.

Szold, Henrietta. "Beruriah," *The Jewish Encyclopedia*, Vol. 3. New York, 1903.

3. DONA GRACIA

Fernand-Halphen, Alice. *Une Grande Dame Juive de la Renaissance: Gracia Mendesia Nasi*. Paris, 1929.

Roth, Cecil. *The House of Nasi: Dona Gracia*. Philadelphia, 1947.

———, *The House of Nasi: The Duke of Naxos*. Philadelphia, 1948.

4. GLUECKEL OF HAMELN

Glueckel of Hameln translated by Beth Zion Abrahams. London, 1962.

Glueckel of Hameln, translated by M. Lowenthal. New York, 1932.

Minkoff, Nahum B. *Glikl Hamel* (Yiddish). New York, 1952.

5. RAHEL VARNHAGEN

Arendt, Hannah. *Rahel Varnhagen. The Life of a Jewish Woman,* translated by Richard and Clara Winston, London, 1957.

Key, Ellen. *Rahel Varnhagen, A Portrait,* translated by Arthur Chuter. New York, 1913.

Mayer, Berta. *Salon Sketches.* New York, 1938, pp. 51-117.

6. REBECCA GRATZ

Marcus, Jacob Rader. *Memoirs of American Jews 1775-1865,* Vol. 1. Philadelphia, 1955, pp. 272-288.

Osterweis, Rollin G. *Rebecca Gratz: A Study in Charm.* New York, 1935.

Philipson, David (ed.) *Letters of Rebecca Gratz.* Philadelphia, 1929.

Biskin, Miriam. *Pattern for a Heroine: The Life Story of Rebecca Gratz.* New York, 1967. (Young Readers)

7. ERNESTINE ROSE

Stanton, E. C., Anthony, S. B., and Gage, M. J. *History of Woman Suffrage,* Vols. I and III. Rochester, 1881-1887.

Suhl, Yuri. *Ernestine P. Rose and the Battle for Human Rights.* New York, 1959.

Williams, Mary Wilhelmine. "Ernestine Louise Siismondi Potowski Rose," *Dictionary of American Biography,* Vol. XVI. New York, 1935.

8. THE MAID OF LUDOMIR

Ashkenazi, Solomon. *Ha-Isha B'Ispaklarit Hayehudit* (Hebrew), Vol. I. Tel Aviv, 1955, pp. 54-56.

Herodetsky, Samuel A. *Leaders of Hasidim,* translated by Maria Herodetsky-Magazanik. London, 1928, pp. 114-117.

Twersky, Johanan. *Ha-Betulah mi-Ludomir* (Hebrew novel). Jerusalem, 1949.

9. RACHEL

Beauvallet, Leon. *Rachel and the New World,* translated by Colin Clair. New York, 1967.

Falk, Bernard. *Rachel the Immortal.* New York, 1936.

Richardson, Joanne. *Rachel.* New York, 1957.

10. HANNAH G. SOLOMON

Solomon, Hannah G. *Fabric of My Life–The Story of a Social Pioneer.* New York, 1974.

The New York Times, December 9, 1942. 27:3.

11. HENRIETTA SZOLD

Fineman, Irving. *Woman of Valor.* New York, 1961.

Levensohn, Lotta. "*Henrietta Szold,*" *American Jewish Yearbook,* Vol. 47 (1945-1946). Philadelphia, pp. 51-70.

Levine, Alexandra L. *The Szolds of Lombard Street.* Philadelphia, 1960.

Zeitlin, Rose. *Henrietta Szold, Record of a Life.* New York, 1952.

12. LILLIAN WALD

Davis, Allen F. *Spearheads for Reform.* New York, 1967

Duffus, Robert L. *Lillian Wald, Neighbor & Crusader,* New York, 1938.

Wald, Lillian. *The House on Henry Street.* New York, 1915.

——, *Windows on Henry Street.* New York, 1933.

Williams, Berl. *Angel of Henry Street*. New York, 1957.

13. EMMA GOLDMAN

Drinnon, Richard. *Rebel in Paradise: A Biography of Emma Goldman*. Chicago, 1961.

Goldman, Emma. *Living My Life*. Vols. 1 and 2. New York, 1931.

Shulman, Alix K. *Red Emma Speaks: Selected Writings and Speeches by Emma Goldman*. New York, 1972

14. HELENA RUBINSTEIN

"Helena Rubinstein," *Current Biography*. 1943, p. 642.

O'Higgins, Patrick. *Madame, An Intimate Biography of Helena Rubinstein*. New York, 1971.

15. SARAH SCHENIRER

Jung, Leo. *Jewish Leaders*. New York, 1953. p. 40.

Kurzweil, Zvi E. *Modern Trends in Jewish Education*. New York, 1964, pp. 266-275.

Schenirer, Sarah. *be-Yisrael-The Writings of Sarah Schenirer* (Hebrew), 3 Vols. Tel Aviv, 1956.

16. GERTRUDE STEIN

Mellow, James R. *Charmed Circle. Gertrude Stein & Co*. New York, 1974.

Stewart, Allegra. *Gertrude Stein & the Present*. Boston, 1967.

Wilson, Ellen. *They Named Her Gertrude Stein* New York, 1973. (Young Readers.)

Winner, Viola Hopkins. "Gertrude Stein," *Dictionary of American Biography*, Supplement 4. New York, 1974, pp. 767-770.

17. NELLY SACHS

Steinbach, A. Allen. "Nelly Sachs—Nobel Laureate," *Jewish*

Book Annual, Vol. 25 (1967-1968). New York, pp. 42-52.

Zohn, Harry. "Nelly Sachs," *Enclyclopaedia Judaica,* Vol. 14. Jerusalem, 1971.

18. ANA PAUKER

"Ana Pauker." *Current Biography* 1948, pp. 493-495. *The New York Times Index.* New York, 1947-1953; 1959

19. LOUISE NEVELSON

Glimcher, Arnold. *Louise Nevelson.* New York, 1972.

MacKown, Diana. *Dawn Plus Dusk.* New York, 1976.

20. DOROTHY SCHIFF

"Dorothy Schiff," Current Biography. 1965, pp. 364-366.

Hellman, Geoffrey. "Dorothy Schiff," *The New Yorker,* August 10, 1968. p. 37ff.

Potter, Jeffrey. *Men, Money & Magic; The Story of Dorothy Schiff.* New York, 1976.

21. ROSALIND FRANKLIN

Olby, Robert. *"Rosalind Elsie Franklin,"* *Dictionary of Scientific Biography,* Vol. V. New York, 1972, pp. 139-142.

Sayre, Anne. *Rosalind Franklin and DNA.* New York, 1975.

Watson, James D. *The Double Helix.* New York, 1965.

22. GOLDA MEIR

Meir, Golda. *A Land of Our Own, An Oral Autobiography,* edited by Maria Syrkin. New York, 1973.

Meir, Golda. *My Life.* New York, 1975.

INDEX

Czechoslovakia, 151
Czernobiel, Rabbi Mordechai of, 70
Czolgosz, Leon, 115

Damascus, Syr., 6
Danzig, 33
Davidson, Jo, 136
Davis, Paulina Wright, 58, 61
Dawn's Wedding Feast, 156
Dayan, Moshe, 178
De La Salle, Jouslin, 73
Denmark, 31
D'Hericourt, Jenny P., 62
Der Magische Taenzer, 145
Dessau, 34
Diaspora, 3, 11
Dimitroff, Georgi, 151
Diogenes, 5
Disraeli, Benjamin, 77
DNA, 169, 173, 174
Dortmund, Ger., 146
Double Helix, The, 169, 176
Douglass, Frederick, 64
Dowry, 36, 37
Dreiser, Theodore, 119
Droste-Hulshoff Award, 146
Duke of Noxos, see Joao Miquez
D'Urquijo, Raphael, 45

Education, 55, 95, 97, 126, 130, 150
Egypt, 77
Eli, Ein Mysterienspeil vom Leiden Israels, 145
Elijah, The Prophet, 71
Ellis, Havelock, 118
Ellis Island, 117
England, 21, 40, 41, 57, 64, 83, 117, 119, 123, 153, 170, 180
Eshkol, Levi, 178
Esther, 74
Eugene, Prince, 143
Europe, 20, 25, 26, 31, 33, 35, 41, 54, 60, 62, 64, 74, 75, 84, 92, 93, 94, 98, 119, 122, 129, 133, 135, 149, 152, 156
Everybody's Autobiography, 139
Ewing, Samuel, 50, 51

Fascism, 120

Federal Association of German Industries, 146
Federation of American Zionists, 94, 95
Felix, Alexandre, 75
 Elisa, see Rachel
 Esther Haya, 72
 Gabriel Victor, 75
 Jacob, 72
 Sarah, 72, 77
Female Hebrew Benevolent Society, 51
Fennos, 50
Ferdinand and Isabella, 18, 19
Ferrara, It., 23
Festivals,
 Purim, 74
 Rosh Hashannah, 180
 Shavuoth, 34
 Tabernacles, 3
 Yom Kippur, 76
Fichte, 43, 45
Finckenstein, Count Carl Von, 43
First Commonwealth, 1
Fitzgerald, F. Scott, 137
Flanders, Belg., 24
Flesch, Rabbi, 127
Florence, It., 23
Flucht und Verwandlung, 145
Foreign Minister, 148, 151, 153, 178, 181
Four In America, 139
Four Saints in Three Acts, 139
France, 21, 22, 23, 41, 46, 57, 74, 75, 77, 119, 123, 139, 140, 151, 153, 172, 175
Franco, General, 139, 156
Frankfurt, Ger., 33, 34, 46, 80
Franklin, Ellis, 169, 170
 Muriel Walley, 169
Franklin, Rosalind, 169-176
Freier, Recha, 100, 101, 103
French, 44, 45, 76, 77, 80, 83, 86, 87, 90, 150, 162
Frick, Henry Clay, 114
Friedrich, Prince, 35, 36
Fuggers, 31

Garches, 136
Gauguin, 135

192